Great
ANGLING
DISASTERS

Great
ANGLING
DISASTERS

Edited by Tom Quinn

Quiller

First published in the UK in 2017
by Quiller, an imprint of Quiller Publishing Ltd

British Library Cataloguing-in-Publication Data
A catalogue record for this book is available
from the British Library

ISBN 978 1 84689 241 7

Cover illustration by John Holder

Printed in Malta

Quiller
An imprint of Quiller Publishing Ltd
Wykey House, Wykey, Shrewsbury, SY4 1JA
Tel: 01939 261616
Email: info@quillerbooks.com
Website: www.quillerpublishing.com

Contents

Introduction

FISHING, it has been said, is an accident waiting to happen. It's not just the inevitable tangles, the hooks caught in bushes (and sometimes ears!) and the occasional tumble into the river. It's also the unpredictability of the fish, the vagaries of the weather and the sheer intractability of the natural world in which we pursue a hobby that non-fishermen find at best eccentric and at worst downright mad.

Given the odds stacked against the fisherman it is amazing, perhaps, that we ever catch anything.

Great days when all goes well are wonderful, certainly, but they are never quite as amusing or memorable as disastrous days. Nothing bonds two fishermen discussing the day's events more than tales of doom and disaster.

This book is the result of a long period of research into more than a century of publishing about fishing. In the second half of the nineteenth century and especially with the development of fly lines that could be cast, there was an explosion in the number of fishing books and journals being published. I have scoured these, as well as early newspapers, in search of the most extraordinary and, I hope, funniest tales of angling disaster. It is these tales you will find collected here and I hope that you will enjoy them as much as your forebears a century and more ago.

The book includes game, coarse and sea fishing and I have been careful to select a range of stories from Britain, Europe, the United States and beyond.

It has always seemed a great pity that the various branches of angling have become so separate. It was not always so. In the nineteenth century and well into the twentieth, salmon fishers were delighted to fish for pike in winter and trout fishermen staying by the sea would often try their hand at mackerel or bass fishing. This book tries to some extent to return to those heady, optimistic days – after all, the excitement of a good bass leaping through the surf is not perhaps that different from a barbel boring downstream or a salmon on its first terrifying rush.

Chapter 1

OVERWHELMED
AND
UNDERPLAYED

Caught in the Flies

GIVEN the amount of casting the average angler gets through in a day it is astonishing that our hospital casualty departments are not permanently full of fishermen asking to have hooks removed from various parts of their anatomy. For the fact is that a fish hook is a nasty piece of equipment if it manages to snare the fisherman rather than his fish.

One man who suffered badly from badly placed hooks was Major F. Powell Hopkins. He was a skilful and enthusiastic fisherman who caught dozens of different species during a long Army career that took him all over the world. In retirement he spent a great deal of time in Ireland, fishing every day for months on end for salmon, trout and sea trout. Despite the fact that he was enormously experienced, he was also rather clumsy, but being convinced that a British officer – even a retired British officer – was always right he tended to blame his long suffering gillie for any mistakes. The gillie got his revenge on one extraordinary day, however.

The two men were out fishing on a lough in the west of Ireland when the major hooked a large salmon. He played the fish for twenty minutes and then drew it toward the gillie's net. It had all seemed so easy up till now. The salmon had fought hard and there had been exciting moments when it might have got off, but it was a relief now to bring it to the net as they were unlikely to get another fish that day. Perhaps it was this knowledge that made the major a little more complacent that he would normally have been. But whatever the reason, he discovered, while the salmon still had several feet to go to reach the net, that he had tied on a very long cast and that the top part of the cast could not be reeled in because the fly on the top dropper had jammed in the top ring of the rod. The major couldn't walk backwards – which is what he would have done if he'd been fishing from the bank – and he had no other options.

He held his rod as high as he could to keep a tight line with the salmon, but he was in a jam and he knew it.

Quick as a flash, he realised there was only one solution. He handed the rod to his gillie and then reached up to grab the cast near the top of the rod. The salmon was tired, which was reassuring, but the major noticed that his hook had only a very light hold on the fish's jaw. He began to pull the fish towards him, hand over hand along the gut cast. With just three feet of line to go before he could get his fingers in the salmon's gills and whip it out, disaster struck.

The salmon had clearly had time to recover a little and, seeing the major bending so close, it decided to make one last bid for freedom. With a flick of its powerful tail – the fish must have weighed nearly twenty pounds – it plunged deep beneath the boat, pulling the cast through the major's hands. It was at this moment that the gillie heard a piercing scream, and on looking across he saw the major hopping about in the end of the boat like a demented thing. The major was also shouting and cursing. He was clearly in great pain, but the gillie was baffled and could see no reason for the fuss. But then he realised what had happened. As the gut had been yanked out of the major's hands, the top fly – the one that had jammed in the rod rings and started all the trouble in the first place – had caught the major in the front of his trousers. From listening to the major's cries, the gillie quickly realised that the hook had not just penetrated the major's trousers in the region of his buttons.

Worse – much worse – the hook had quite clearly hooked something highly sensitive inside the major's trousers. By this time the major was howling in pain and dancing a curious jig. He'd managed to catch hold of the cast again to stop the tugs of the salmon inflicting even more pain and injury on him, but the gut was cutting the major's hands. It was the only time in his life that the major had wished desperately to lose a fish, but despite everything the gut held and the salmon continued to thrash on the end of the line.

In the instant the gillie realised what had happened he involuntarily laughed. Incensed, the major took a swing and boxed the gillie with his free hand. The punch winded the gillie, who fell awkwardly into the back of the boat. The violent rocking caused by the fall made the salmon panic and the major's hands and groin began to suffer again.

It took five minutes for the gillie to get back on his feet and cut the line. The major sat silent and scowling as the gillie rowed them back to the bank. He was furious with the gillie, but knew that the story would be all over the village if he did not apologise for his behaviour. At last the solution came to him. He offered a gillie a full bottle of whisky on condition that not a word of the day's affair was breathed to anyone. The gillie shook on it and the two men agreed to meet again in the morning for another day on the lough.

Robert Storey, *Days of My Youth,* 1898

Caught in a Drain

FOLLOWING the poaching of a large number of salmon by night spearing, police arrested a notorious local character, John Brennan. Brennan had previously been involved in a number of unlicensed salmon fishing expeditions, to the great detriment of the fishery.

He presented no defence in court but there was much laughter at his expense when the arresting officer gave evidence. Constable Robinson explained that Brennan was of such low intelligence that, despite his repeated failures, he thought of himself as a far superior to his honest neighbours; he believed, said Robinson, that he could trick the police and vanish at will from anyone pursuing him. His absolute certainty of his own mental superiority had been his undoing.

The constable went on to describe how Brennan had on a previous occasion used foul hooking tackle to 'sniggle' one of the biggest salmon ever seen in the river. Having landed the huge fish, he cut it into pieces before remembering that there was a good cash prize offered by a local publican for the biggest fish in a year from the river. Brennan was so enraged at his own stupid mistake that he determined to return to the river as often as he could in the hope of catching another record-breaker.

On a previous poaching summons to court Brennan – described by the policeman as short and very fat – had tried to escape the police by hiding in a drain near the town bridge. His portly frame ensured that once in the drain Brennan could not get out again and he spent the rest of the night crying for help, which came at last in the form of the constable who had chased him from the river the previous evening. Fined twenty shillings.

Northumberland Gazette, October 1890

A Fortune Lost

CUCUMBERS, pineapples, two pheasants, and probably some other delicacies of the kind cultivated by the enthusiastic amateur are notoriously expensive to the producer, but I doubt whether man ever paid so much for his fancy as I had to pay for a certain salmon hooked and lost in a river, let me say, not one hundred miles from the Grampian Hills.

So near as I can approximate the business, I paid exactly five hundred and twenty-one pounds and some odd shillings and pence for the privilege of losing that miserable fish (roughly £30,000 in 2016, Ed).

The experience fell to my lot during one of many confidential expeditions for the eminent firm which it is my pleasure to serve, and for a while I believed I had been cured once for all of what my friends were pleased to term my madness for angling.

And it happened in this wise.

I had been sent abroad upon an extremely delicate and private mission. By my cuteness and knowledge of human frailty, to say nothing of my learnedness in legal matters, I could say without egotism that I had saved a member of the Upper House whose name it would not become me to mention not only a considerable amount of property but also a scandal.

I was hurried away on the night mail to the client's castle to inform him in detail of the final and satisfactory upshot of my inquiries and negotiations. He was becomingly grateful, and made me a present the like of which I had never before had. Indeed, he was so profuse in his gratitude that, hearing in course of conversation that I loved fishing, he placed his river at my disposal.

At this period, I had chambers that I shared with a cousin in Gray's Inn, and towards the end of January, finding myself in the possession of a balance at the Birkbeck Bank, at which I had opened an account with all the pride of a man finding himself for the first time in his life in possession of a cheque book, I resolved to have a little holiday. Should it take the form of fishing, or shooting, or travelling?

It was all over with grouse, and deer stalking was out of the question. Should I hire a small yacht, and cruise around the Essex or Hampshire shores on the lookout for wildfowl, or should I equip myself at one of the London tackle makers, and hie me northwards in time for the opening of the February salmon fishing season?

All things considered, I resolved upon the latter course and, remembering the permission I had received, sent a note to the steward to whom I had been directed to announce my intentions whenever I thought of visiting the place, stating that I should be there on the opening day of the season.

It was now that began the expenses to which I referred in the opening paragraph of this essay. Fifteen shillings went without loss of time for a well-known standard work on angling; three guineas soon followed for a salmon rod, which I was assured would answer all my purposes. Several shillings went in traces and flies; several pounds for winch and line; and a rather heftier sum for a return ticket to the station in north Britain that would land me at the nearest point to the castle. It was a bold and stupid thing for me to do, who, until then, had never used a salmon rod, and had never, except by accident while trout fishing once in Ireland, caught a salmon, as to which I may plead the excuse urged by a well-known heroine of fiction, and say that it was a very small one.

The river, however, to which I was bound was a notoriously good early salmon river, but a very difficult one to fish. The banks were, at the part that I had at my disposal, generally high, and the stream rapid and rough, difficult to command under any circumstances, but especially difficult when a hooked salmon left no alternative but to follow the game pell mell downstream.

We had had no snow in England, but there had been, as usual, an abundance of it on the Scottish mountains; when I arrived by the river I was told that the bulk of the snow had gone, and that although the river was much clearer than it had been, my chances of catching a fish were extremely small.

Nothing daunted, the opening day found me at nine o'clock in the morning at the riverside, attended by the young gillie, who was himself an adept at angling, and who could quickly see with half a glance that I knew nothing whatever about this branch of the sport.

It took him an hour at least to initiate me into the mystery of handling the long, heavy rod and throwing the fly decently, and before twelve o'clock had arrived I can promise you my shoulders ached and my arms seemed as if they would drop from my body. I have since discovered that, had the river been like the Tweed, or Tay, or Dee, I might have had a better chance, because the theories I had formed from a close study of the angling book that I had purchased to read on my downward journey would have enabled me to command the pools and more easily fishable streams with which those rivers abound. The Spey cast was unknown to me then but I had very little chance with this tumbling and roaring stream, casting, as I had to do, from the aforesaid high banks. There was one bit of comparatively tractable water on the opposite side of the river where it narrowed previous to taking a sharp sweep, and plunging on between rocks. It was a dark rolling pool, upon which I felt certain I could pitch the fly given me by the gillie, and which he called the Beauty – a very handsome arrangement, with a massive many-hued wing, an orange head and a body of green, ribbed with gold.

To my delight Sandy, after moving down the bank and looking intently across at the pool, announced that he had seen the movement of a salmon.

We consulted hopefully, and, receiving from him instructions to be careful to keep myself cool, to make a leisurely yet decisive cast, and not to have out too much line, I succeeded in dispatching the fly fairly well to the head of the pool. I had by this time learned how the fly was to be humoured, although the downstream method and the working of the fly up and down seemed to me a much clumsier proceeding than the delicate operations to which I had been used with a 10ft single-handed rod and the light tackle employed upon trout in our Southern streams.

At the fourth cast I felt, not what I can exactly describe as a rise or strike, but a sudden checking of the fly, and while wondering what had happened the line tightened, the rod bent, the winch began to revolve, and I experienced the delight of having hooked an expected salmon. It was lucky for me that I had not been aware at the first movement that I had a fish on the hook, because I am tolerably sure that if I had known it, I should have struck wildly, and very likely wrenched the fly from its mouth. However, it seemed all right, and I had a good deal of hard work with that fish. He was at first disinclined to leave the safe shelter of the pool, but the salmon rod was undoubtedly more equal to the work than I was myself and by keeping it fairly well up and allowing the pliant top to do the rest I at any rate did not destroy my chances.

At some point of the riverside lower down there were obstacles the best angler in the world could not have overcome, especially as at those parts the water was so deep that wading would have been impossible; but my starting place happened to be the most favourable at which a tyro like myself could have commenced operations, and I do not pretend to arrogate to myself much credit for following the fish cautiously downstream, and ultimately bringing it within reach of Sandy's ready clip, at a rock where further progress was barred. However, almost at the end of battle, just when victory was in sight, I took my eyes from the point where the line entered the water, the fish slipped further downstream and the line parted with a crack.

During the rest of my sojourn upon the noble river, not another sign of fish did I observe. The wealthy gentleman who was owner of the policies was not in residence at this time, and his steward informed me that he was spending the winter in the south of France, and would probably not return until Easter.

I may add another sovereign to the expenses that I have enumerated above.

Returning to town, and taking a cab from Euston to the narrow and somewhat dingy thoroughfare that was doomed before long to be, if not removed from the face of the earth, at least widened and made more worthy of a great metropolis, I was struck by the absence of anyone in the sitting room that my cousin Harry and myself occupied, and there was an air of desertion about the chambers, never perhaps very bright, which struck me with a peculiar sensation of gloom. The fires were unkindled, and, to make the story short, no Harry appeared that night, nor indeed the next morning. I may go so far as to state that a whole fortnight passed without my hearing any tidings of that lost and silent relation and bosom friend.

Things appeared to be getting serious, and I had already taken preliminary steps towards advertising the truant, when I received a letter from him that I may conscientiously say was a remarkable one. It staggered me on the spot. It was dated from Liverpool, some days previous to the morning upon which I received it, and it began by asking me, for old acquaintance' sake, to forgive him – him who had ever been a pattern of youthful exuberance and honesty.

He said he had a crime to confess, and all that was left for him was at the earliest opportunity to make what he had the impudence to call restitution. It seems that while I had been enjoying my fishing, the client I had thought in the south of France called to see me at my chambers. My cousin Harry explained that I was in Scotland, and my client inquired whether he could do anything for Harry on my account during my absence. The distinguished visitor then, having been assured by my plausible cousin that there were no secrets between us, and that what was confidential to one might be considered as confidential to the other, informed him that the lady who, I may whisper, was at the bottom of all the trouble which had cast a cloud over his life and house for the previous two years, had met him at Nice, and that the result of their interview was an additional flow of appreciation for my good offices. In short, my client had come to my chambers to ask my acceptance of a cheque, upon which three figures were written – the amount being, to dissemble no longer, the, to me, magnificent sum of £500. A true-hearted and genial gentleman this worthy client certainly was, but much too innocent, and much too confiding in others, I should say, to be allowed much control over financial matters. Otherwise he surely would never have been induced, plausible as my cousin was, and no doubt still remains, to have handed over to him the open cheque, the glorious present intended for myself.

But he did so, with a neat speech, as I have since heard, and Harry, the good trusted, and suave, I regret to say, now wrote from Liverpool, to the effect that he had never sinned before and never would sin again. He explained, in a nicely turned sentence, in which he was mighty particular about a certain semicolon, that he had never had as much money in hand before, and that the worthy nobleman had specially tempted him by not crossing the cheque or placing any other restriction upon its administration.

The absconder very calmly, and in unexceptionable grammar, pointed out that the gift was unexpected by me and was altogether to be regarded as 'an extra', and that therefore I would probably agree with him that the appropriation was no great loss. Still, he was sorry, and had betaken himself to that convenient refuge of all honest persons on the other side of the Atlantic, intending, as he grimly put it, to begin the world anew with something like a chance in his favour.

And this precious cousin finished with a cool, 'You would have done the same under the circumstances, my boy, and whether you forgive me or not I shall always remain your sincere well-wisher, Harry.'

I may add that in a postscript the writer explained that he resisted the temptation for four-and-twenty hours and then felt compelled – compelled to forge an endorsement, cash the cheque, and make tracks.

The theft of that £500, the great expense to which I had been put on my journey to Scotland, the determination that, after sore communing with myself, I came to allow the thing to go by without attempting to pursue the runaway thief, hit me extremely hard for the time.

Added to my other losses, I may state that that disastrous fishing trip deprived me for a long time of a pleasure that had lightened many an hour of my life; for I swore by all the gods never again to take rod in hand, or to indulge in that delightfully gentle art that would only serve to remind me of the dishonesty of one whom I had treated as a brother, and of the loss, for the sake of a few days fishing, of what to me would have been a fortune.

Red Spinner, A Mixed Bag, 1895

Mystery Fish

WE ROWED out on to the lake at dawn. It was June, warm and sultry and the season barely open a week. The three of us were ready and fully ready for the giant tench we knew lurked in the quiet corners of this most inaccessible lake. We planned to fish where only a boat could reach and as this was a lake where no one had fished for many years, we had high hopes of a big bag.

Dark impenetrable woods came down to the water's edge wherever we looked and the water had an eerie stillness. Not a breath of wind stirred.

It was so still that when we began to fish there seemed no need to anchor the boat. We baited our spot with breadcrumb and worms, threaded worms on to our hooks and waited.

All was still. Twenty minutes after we had started John's float vanished. He struck. The rod curved deep towards the water. 'I think I'm snagged,' said John. He tried everything to free his line but without success but, just when he had decided to pull for a break, the fish – if fish it was – began to move. It swam steadily away from the boat; no lunges, no head shaking; only a smooth heavy determination to get as far from the boat and us as possible. Perhaps it was a carp, but John had played many large carp and insisted this was something else.

He could do nothing with the fish so we rowed in the direction it had taken us. John was almost out of line. We were both excited and slightly fearful. The fish stopped dead and skulked on the bottom. We came to a halt almost directly above where the fish lay. Then John made a mistake. He stood up the better to play the fish should it make another run. When we least expected it, that's just what the fish did. It set off at speed, taking us all by surprise, and in his haste to get into a good position to play the fish, John tripped and crashed over the side of the boat into ten feet of murky water. He tried to keep in contact with the fish but the water was cold and we had to help John out quickly; by the time we fished him out and picked up his rod that huge fish was gone.

We set off for home having agreed that this was our worst start to a fishing season ever.

The Angler Magazine, August 1906

The End of the Legendary Grayling

ROOKE had never heard of anything more stupendous. On this head I offered suggestions, and it was because of the deferential attention paid to imparted information concerning the reputed monsters of continental waters, and the more or less authentic records of 4lb, and even 5lb, grayling in England, that I found myself becoming at last as much interested in this celebrity of the Dale as any of my hearers.

I accordingly sent for rod, flies, and wading trousers, and determined, if there should be a suitable day during my visit, to try for the fish that, it was believed, could never be caught.

At first the weather was wet and most unseasonably mild; there were polyanthuses and other flowers a bloom, and everything promised a green, churchyard-filling season. But suddenly one wild December night, with a change of moon, the wind veered round into the nor-norwest, and honest winter set in, not as it so often does with two or three white frosts, but with a determined black one from the very commencement. The water, therefore, in a short time waned below its average level, and ran in pristine clearness. For a whole week the sun shone and in the midday hours, after getting through my correspondence and some arrears of entry that I had brought with me, I devoted myself to a systematic study of the river. I invited Rooke to show me the big grayling. This was a mile and a half upstream from the Duke's Arms.

It was among the most picturesque scenery, and where the hoary rocks, with all the signs of centuries of weather, frowned upon the stream. Past the parsonage, about a mile on the way, we pushed on through a gorge, where the deep black current was confined within limestone walls not more than ten yards apart. On the other side of a plantation of larches, some distance further, the river expanded to its normal average of twenty-five yards. Then it began to widen out after the manner of a bottle, and for a couple of furlongs it was a broad sheet of quite fifty yards from shore to shore. There was a prominent cliff, not of rock but of sand, on the side where the footpath lay, and, halting here amid the hollies, mountain ashes, and an undergrowth that grew over the very edge of the top, Rooke pointed down and said, 'That's where he lives, sir.'

The river ran, as near as could be guessed, forty feet below this bank, which was precipitous, and it seemed possible that the big grayling – if this indeed was his haunt – had seldom been fished for. The only way of reaching him, apparently, was from the other side, where, it is true, the ground was reasonably sloping, although there was a good deal of foliage from trees and bushes to be avoided. As could be seen at a glance, it would require little less than fifty yards to reach the fish with a fly rod.

Fishing from our forty-foot hill was out of the question and, as for a boat, there was no such in the district.

The water had been from the outset represented by both the landlord and Rooke as very deep. In this sombre, slowly gliding pool, the stream, such as it was, meandered around past the point where the fish lay, leaving a contracted lay-by under the rock. It was a space of harbourage that might have been covered with a blanket, and the course that distinguished the stream from the eddy was always marked by a pretty dotting of white foam. On the first day of inspection I noticed two cock-winged flies sailing down and observed that they were gently drifted out of the current into the eddy, where they remained uneasily shifting for a little while; then the stream would claim re-possession, entice them gradually out, and bear them away.

This was obviously the quiet haven that a fly-taking fish would select and maintain against all comers, and where, if any accident happened to the tenant in possession, another would immediately succeed him. It was the sort of situation in life that human beings are often on the look-out for − an easy refuge into which providence will bring food and sustenance without any trouble, and at somebody else's expense. An observing angler would not be long in deciding that he could only proceed here scientifically.

In reply to a question as to whether anyone had ever fished from the bank or otherwise with a worm or gentle, Rooke related a long story of attempts that had been made within his remembrance. The first was that of a flash and rash young man from London who pooh-poohed the idea of not being able to fish out this giant historical grayling and at his own motion he sallied forth one September afternoon to teach the natives the trick. He was armed with a general rod, and the hook was baited with finely baked wasp grub, but he came to trouble in the preliminaries, for, in his efforts to let the bait down from the top of the high bank, he so strove and stretched to keep the line free from the bushes, that he lost his foothold, fell head over heels into the stream, smashed up rod and tackle, and would probably have been drowned but that he was a strong swimmer. He floundered ashore on the further bank, and the disastrous adventure seemed to have sickened him; he made no further attempts, and the story of the mishap became worked up at last into a fearsome tradition as to the perils of the place. Henceforth, a touch of mystery began to incrust the spirit of the locality, acting occasionally as a superstition to scare the very susceptible. Sometime after the young man from London had thus shown the natives how not to succeed, a Nottingham angler became fired with holy zeal, and, laughing superstition to scorn, and making light of all difficulties and previous failed attempts and disasters, came gallantly into the Dale in quest of the big grayling. He, however, knew something of the game to be played, reconnoitred the spot like a general, and decided to have nothing to with the high bank and the forty-foot drop. Relying in trustful confidence upon his power of casting from the reel, he planned an attack from the other side, and after sundry trials, the man of Trent cast his red worm and shotted float-line across in a workmanlike style.

At this mighty out-throw the worthy Rooke and his son drawn up in reserve near the angler volubly offered tributes of admiration and saw with satisfaction that the float swam delicately in the eddy itself. Nor had much time elapsed ere they all saw that float tremble, slant aside and disappear, and they were in an instant galvanised into excitement at the bend of the rod and the rush downstream of the hooked fish. Here then was their old friend at last!

It must be a monster indeed and naturally enough on a small hook and fine tackle, it was master of the situation. The incidents of the memorable fight that ensued were so circumstantially told that I accepted them as probably true. As it proceeded the story became downright amusing.

Rooke declared that the fish led them a punishing race right away down to the vicarage and that not one of the trio had a glimpse of it for more than an hour.

Two or three of the vicar's visitors were looking out over the lawn when the angler with his bent rod and the keeper and his son hove into view and the parson knew quite well that the shouting signified sport abroad.

By the time therefore that the fisherman and his attendants had reached the lawn that slopes to the riverside, from which it is only separated by a gravel path, there was an appreciative audience of ladies and gentlemen to watch the issue.

The big fish was now, however, showing signs of weariness and the angler was in a state of perspiration, hope and fear, but disaster was soon to overwhelm all his efforts.

He walked backwards up the gravel spit that marked the boundary between lawn and kitchen garden, and as he retired in good order the heavy fish at the end of the line followed the steady strain. A gardener ran down breathless with a landing net at the nick of time, but what came out of the water in its capacious pocket was not the long hoped for record-breaking grayling but a monstrous eel of six and a half pounds.

The gardener, backing hastily into the garden with his burden and catching sight of the hideous brute wriggling in its slime within the meshes, completely lost his head, turned the net upside down and shot the eel out into a small bed of savoury herbs and parsley. The vicaress, good lady, shrieked a warning that added to the general confusion.

The eel then began to bound about and work his way where the summer growths were choicest. The three men who were trying to get their foot upon its head fled before the writhing advance and soon became panic stricken. Even two of the visitors, having never seen such a creature before, took to their heels and blindly rushed across a much-prized asparagus bed, trampling the young shoots fore and aft with liberal impartiality.

The fisherman himself shared the passing madness, for he seemed not to care about his game now that he had it at his feet, but jumped around anxious only to save his rod and keep the line tight. The effort, however, to prevent the gut being twisted up with the eel robbed him of the remnant left of his presence of mind and he went backwards plump through a cucumber frame and on backwards through the glass of the garden doors. Pandemonium was everywhere.

The vicar and his daughter now came into action, perceiving that the border of old-fashioned flowers, which was the special pride of the young lady's sister, was being irretrievably ravaged by the furious tramping and running. At length a stable help arrived with an implement that was not unlike a mattock, and hacked the eel on and about the head; then the tumult was allayed, and the damage to vegetables and flowers reckoned up, and duly deplored and apologised for. The eel was cut up and distributed as a choice morsel, and the memory of the attempts made by the recipients to eat that coarse flesh has survived along with the sensational progress of the capture.

As it happened, this invasion of the vicarage grounds was a very unpleasant coincidence. That big grayling, I should fancy, was a tabooed subject in this peaceful household, as it was associated with an unpleasant chapter in its history.

Two or three years previously, a young relative, who had been called to the bar, had heard or read of the champion grayling of the Dale, came to the vicarage for a fishing holiday previous to the winter work of the courts, and set upon trying for the prize. But he fell in love with a lady on the journey, devoted his time to riding to and with her, eloped with her from the town over the hills, and figured in the Division reports as an inmate of the vicarage. Of this scandal the great fish was, in a measure, the indirect cause.

The grayling was, however, still reported to be in his haunt, and there he was when I, as before described, appeared upon the scene. It took me nearly four days to make a chart of the bed of the river, and I happened upon a discovery that pleased me much; looking from the top of the bank, just where the neck of the bottle begins to widen out, I saw that in the very centre of the pool was a gravelly spit about thirty feet long and two yards wide, narrowing at the upper end to a point that was nearly abreast of the whereabouts to be mastered.

If I could wade up to this shelf, there was only a cast of about twenty yards between me and the grayling. After marking well the vantage ground, I re-examined the stream below through the neck of the bottle, and eventually saw a probable way, by wading in from the other side, and adopting a serpentine route, to gain the desired point.

This I duly essayed. The landlord and his son, Rooke and his son, two natives who had heard of the grand attempt, and the mulled-beer farmer happened on the eventful date to be agreed upon a holiday free from the harassing duties of common life. They had been feasting during the forenoon, and were in good condition therefore, to moralise and play the part of applauding spectators. There was no sun unfortunately, but I felt sure of my map-making, and resolved, whatever came of it to zig-zag in the stream from the other side until I reached the gravel spit. By never moving the hindermost foot until the forward one was firmly planted and by taking ample time, I succeeded in disappointing the expectancies of the lookers-on; they had unanimously decided I should have to be rescued from a watery grave. It would have been an awkward position truly had any accident happened, for in wading trousers a man in a quandary is heavily hampered.

To guard against possibilities, the landlord's son had been furnished with a long rope, to which was tied the broken handle of a pitchfork. It was all properly arranged that, if I was carried away by the stream, or lost my footing, the apparatus should be hurled out upon the water for my benefit. All in good order, I reached the gravel spit, where after all I found myself only to the middle, although in getting to that point I had been twice immersed to the armpits. The depth of the water, I now discovered, had been really exaggerated, as is often the case.

I had been assured by all these men, who had known the river from boyhood, that wading anywhere near the place was an absolute impossibility and madness; but I had relied and acted confidently on my own judgment, with this so far satisfactory result.

The snow was slowly falling when I began to get out line for the cast, and, for the first time during the whole investigations, I saw a fish rising in that eddy. Rooke, stationed on the cliff to signal if necessary, pronounced the riser to be the identical grayling; he knew it by a patch of grey aft the great dorsal fin. Although I had determined to make my first application with a honey-dun bumble, fished wet, upon seeing an unmistakable rise as I stood there in mid-stream, I changed the hackle for a ginger quill, and after waiting for about ten minutes and getting picturesquely whitened by the light flakes and my hands rendered blue with the cold, there was a second rise. The first cast of the fly was outside the eddy; the stream claimed it at once. I recovered it, dried it well, and this time sent it to the correct place, and, without any more ado, the big grayling was hooked.

The landing net, which had been suspended from my shoulder, received the fish after a not very resolute

resistance and, the captor stepping out on his own side, the party of spectators, minus the watchman Rooke, gathered around to see the monster.

Long as I may live I shall never forget the looks of mingled horror, sadness, and confusion expressed on the faces of these good fellows when they saw that their wonderful fish brought down the index not at four pounds, but at exactly two pounds and one ounce. In truth, I have ever since severely regretted the capture of that fish, that cause of broken glass, and failed attempts.

My success robbed the Dale of an article of faith that was most beautiful in itself and harmless in its influence. For a generation the honest natives had boasted of their four pound grayling; they had vaunted it to visitors season after season. Even at the country houses at parties it was cited in opposition to the generally accepted theory that very large grayling only exist in the southern streams.

Children had been taught from their earliest days that their native Dale received glory and honour from the four pound grayling. The landlord and his son at the Duke's Arms had believed in it implicitly; the middle-aged farmer had cherished it as the apple of his eye; and Rooke the keeper existed, as it were, upon it. And now, by yielding to the miserable ambition of catching a solitary grayling, I had brought desolation and an uprooting of faith into an innocent neighbourhood.

Red Spinner, A Mixed Bag, 1895

Chapter 2

BAMBOOZLED

Floundering

ANOTHER memorable fish to be taken on a fly fell to my lot on a dry-fly stream in Gloucestershire two summers before the Great War. I had received a permit for his private water from the last Lord Fitzhardinge, and had had a pretty good day with the mayfly; my bag including a useful three-pounder during the evening rise, and a swallow that took a green drake on the wing during the luncheon interval, when my rod was stuck in the ground and the three-yard cast was blowing out on a strong gale of wind!

When returning upstream at dusk, I met the lessee of the water above. He begged me to try for a big trout in a long pool ending in a stickle before I gave up, and suggested a white moth as the appropriate lure. He was anxious, he said, to take a decent fish home for breakfast.

On reaching the spot, I found that the pool lay at the foot of a steep, high bank and that it was much overhung. I consented to try three casts and then leave it, as it was nearly dark and I had a long way to go home.

Nothing happened, and after the third cast I carelessly let the white moth, a rough fly of my own tying, go on into the stickle before beginning to reel in. As my finger touched the handle I felt a rise and struck. At once I knew I had hooked something very big, and sang out: 'By Jove! I've got your big trout!' The owner hurried up in great excitement, seized the landing net and clambered down the bank. There was a terrific struggle in the dark water, and I began to think I had got into the biggest trout that ever was seen, to quote Mr Jorrocks again.

Gradually I brought the fish to the net and my friend landed it. 'Well, I'm blowed,' he cried, 'Your giant trout, your trout of a lifetime is a bloomin' flounder!' And a flounder it was, and, moreover, foul-hooked through the back fin, or what would have been the back fin in a respectable freshwater fish.

This occurred on the Matford Brook some three miles from the Severn, and there were two or three weirs up which this salt-water flatfish must have made its way before reaching the spot where it was caught. Its weight was well above two pounds. But imagine my disappointment!

Lewis Charles Jewell, *Rod, Pole and Perch,* 1928

No Luck in Ireland

THE SITUATION explained itself when I learned that, just ten days before, the west side mountains had come in for a thunderstorm and flood that let the fish up in shoals so that while we were blaspheming against the drought he had the best of the fishing.

That afternoon, however, I could do nothing but fish over what seemed to be likely rises, changing flies and doing all I knew. In one of the intervals a big fish jumped clean out on the far side of the pool and my gillie looked at him ruefully.

'What weight would you give him?' He said. 'Twenty to five-and-twenty,' I said, 'and I never expected to see the like of him here.'

'I was thinking thirty,' said Maurice glumly, 'and he's been there since May. I tried him with fly and I tried him with worm, and I could do nothing with him.'

I should explain that half a mile or so of the left bank of the Owengariff, comprising four of the best pools, is free fishing, and that my gillie was a professional angler with all the dignity of a licence, taken out for the first time this year. It had bred in him derision for the free fishers.

During all of June he caught no fish, and, as he said, 'the boys were codding me' but the flood came at last and he got seven in the week on this bit of water, showing a handsome profit on the sovereign he paid to fish. A fine fisher he was (as I saw when he took my rod), and the son of a fine old poacher and fly-tier – some of whose flies I commissioned him to bring me. It saddened me to find that all his experience threw doubts on the chance of catching white trout in the tide-pools and, having tried it ineffectually, I went back discouraged to the hotel. Here I found other anglers, one of whom sallied out with me next morning: a dark wet day with a south-easterly breeze, making a fine ripple. Yet I could stir nothing in the big pool, nor in another fine deep stretch above it, and my mind was to leave the water early and get home in good time.

It seemed worthwhile, however, to try first a lower pool, which Maurice had dismissed as too shallow, and here I rose at once what I took to be a sea trout. Persevering, I covered the water to the far side and there at last came most unexpectedly a big swirl. Nothing happened, however, and the fish did not show again. I went down to the stretch below, communing hard with myself, for it was close on the limit of my time if I was to catch the earlier train from Ballyglen, and the drizzle of rain had wetted me completely and I had no means of changing. Still, I had risen a salmon, for the first time this summer; the day was yet young and had many chances. And then, as I looked back, I saw the back of a fish come out lower down in the same hole, where a slight, hardly perceptible swirl in the water had followed my flies.

I went back, fished over the pool carefully, and again on the far side came the heavy rise – and this time my line went down. Jubilantly I raised the point of the rod, the line tightened clear. I saw a great slab of a white side turn over and then the flies fell slack.

Everyone who has fished for salmon knows that sickening feeling, but the man who has fished for salmon at leisure and with ample opportunity knows little of what the disappointment it is to us unfortunates who snatch a hurried chance in a townsman's holiday.

I was in Donegal all of August 1902 and never once straightened the line on what I knew to be a salmon; hardly anyone did through the whole county in that month. Now my chance was gone, and when was it going to come back to me? What is more, the experienced and constant angler knows at least whether he is or is not to blame for a mishap of this kind; the less expert are visited with remorse unknown to him. My soul reproached me that I had not struck harder; even with small flies my little trout rod might have needed a sharper snatch to drive home the barb. And again, your veteran has his proceedings reduced to a formula; he knows exactly what to do when a salmon rises. But for the angler whose experience is chiefly with trout, a salmon's rise is full of pitfalls. If you strike at once, as at a trout, you generally lift the fly from his slow jaws, and the result, at least in my case, is a sudden stiffening of the muscles to prevent the normal reaction to the sight of a rise. Consequently, when I do raise my rod, I raise it slow and cautious as a man does, in short with a very rare chance. But your angler who hooks or rises salmon every other day through the season is free from these tremors and perplexities – the most real that I know. Nevertheless, I had risen a salmon, and all but hooked a salmon – evidently one's duty was to stick to it. That fish was gone. But as I fished down the hole, over the other that I saw rising, again there came the slight swirl, and on a second offer, a full rise.

Mr Lang has somewhere written an admirable ballad about the 'Salmo irritans'. This was a specimen. The brute of a grilse kept me fishing over him at intervals for, I suppose, an hour, rising every now and then but never taking any of the many flies I offered. At last, thinking to circumvent him I crossed the river and tried him from the other side. But it was no good.

Maurice arrived angling on his own account, fished over him. Still no good. My acquaintance from the hotel came down the river from the upper water and reported that that also was no good. Then, while Maurice was busy at the big pool from the free bank, I went to the hole above, put my flies in under the holy bush that gives it a name and suddenly there was a rush and a race, and at the long last I was into a fish.

I 'let a roar out of me' to Maurice, thanking heaven that I was in reach of a big net, for I myself had only a trout net. But the rest of my kit was trout tackle, and though my twelve-foot rod could be trusted, I had doubts as to the little reel. And sure enough, when the fish came in with a run towards me, it was wholly impossible to wind fast enough; the bank was steep behind, and in haste I gathered the line with my hand. That manoeuvre is well enough in a boat, or on smooth ground; but this bank was far from smooth, and when the fish started to run back again I discovered that the coils had been shed into a whin bush. Tearing off lumps of the prickly stuff, and running to the farthest point available, I managed to check the rush without disaster; then with a hasty left hand disentangled the line and by the time Maurice had reached me I was on level terms again. But the suspense lasted for another while, for although the fish showed small, he was big enough for that rod and tackle, and when at last he turned just in front of me, I thought, 'At last a salmon and I'm going to get him.' But at the very moment of my triumph came the anguish: a ping and the fly flew into the air, the salmon slowly righted himself and sank back into the depths.

Stephen Gwynn, *Fishing Holidays*, 1904

Rotten Line

EVEN WORSE is the case in which you hook a good fish, play it for some time, and then see the frayed gut give way. Just as you are bringing the fish to the net, the moment of greatest strain in all the struggle, the salmon half floats, half rolls back to safety.

The worst crime of all, however, is that of neglecting to dry your line thoroughly after use, and almost as bad is that of failing to test both reel, line and backing on a reel that is being used for the first time after being laid aside at the end of the previous season.

It is to this last, and least excusable, piece of carelessness that I must ascribe the minor tragedy that I am about to relate.

Once again it was August, and I had crossed the North Sea and left the Tasso at Christiansund, not on this occasion bound not for Sundal, but for Todal, which lies on the other side of the long peninsula bounding the Sundal Fjord on the north.

The Todal River, which falls into a little bay on the south-west of Sundal, is only a short reach for salmon and sea trout, as a mighty foss, which comes thundering down a narrow gorge some three miles above the sea, presents an effective obstacle that no fish could possibly surmount. Below this, however, runs the little river, with plenty of salmon pools, some natural, some artificial, and all of them the more attractive since, with a reasonable amount of wading, they can be fished from the bank with quite a small rod. My own favourite was a stiff eleven-foot split cane made by Hardy, and carrying a disproportionately large winch holding one hundred and fifty yards of stout backing in addition to forty yards of reel line.

One year I rented Todal myself, but on this occasion I was the guest of my, friend Lord Phillips, for a short but blissful fortnight. The early part of the season had been hot, and most of the lower snow had melted, so that we were dependent on rain for a much needed flood. The river was, in fact, very low, and there had been no fresh run of either salmon or sea trout for some time.

For a day or two we amused ourselves with the brown trout in the upper stretches above the foss, or by sea fishing in the fjord, where, in the clear water, we could see plenty of good fish only waiting for their opportunity of getting up the stream.

On the third night the rain came down with a vengeance as we were smoking our after dinner pipes, so we turned in early to dream of good sport on the morrow. Next morning, we could already see from the veranda that the river had risen nearly two feet, and, as the sticks and rubbish on the bank indicated that the water was falling, all signs pointed to the probability of a successful day. My host started for the upper water; the pools immediately around the house were left for his wife, most skilful and accomplished of lady anglers; and I had the rest of the river down to the sea, an arrangement that, after brawling down a length of shallow rapids, was mostly easy for a wader to cover with a moderate cast.

I threaded my path through a little thicket of alders that fringed the first pool, waded in as far as a well-known boulder that marks the head of it, and began to cast with every hope of success, for the water looked in perfect condition. Almost immediately something powerful took me deep under water, and the line began to run out very deliberately with a strong, even, strain straight down the middle of the river and without the slightest check or intermission.

It was not the swift, impetuous rush of a grilse of sea trout, but the even, deliberate progress of something much larger, and I felt thankful that I had nearly two hundred yards of strong backing behind the reel line. As my fish got farther and farther away, I was all the time edging cautiously towards the bank, where I could have followed it more quickly. Alas! There was no need. When the salmon had got a little more than a hundred yards away, the line, without any increased strain or sudden jerk, parted, the rod straightened, and I was left helpless, minus fish, reel line, cast, fly, and some seventy yards of backing. Depressed and conscience-stricken, I seated myself beside the pool and, doing what I ought to have done before starting to fish, tested the remnant of damaged silk, which snapped like packthread at every pull.

What probably happened was that the boatmen whose duty it was to wind the used line on the drier, had confined their attentions to the first hundred yards, so that the remainder, wound damp on the reel, had gone all to pieces when put away at the end of the season. There was nothing to be done but to recognise that I had paid the price of my carelessness, to shoulder my useless rod and empty net, and to tramp wearily home in my waders.

F. G. Aflalo, *A Book of Fishing Stories,* 1913

American Escapades

THE WEATHER was turning cold – the month was October – and the fish were somewhat sluggish, it appeared. But in the course of time I rose a fish, obviously a trout; then hooked something strong and lively, and played for five minutes or more, and finally landed a beautiful five pound rainbow trout, a perfect picture of a fish in shape and colour.

A day or two after the capture of my first rainbow trout, I learned that there were heavy fish in the Platte. Jim Deacon, the factotum at the Pick Ranch, had somewhere picked up an old Jock Scott salmon fly with a length of gut attached, and pressed me to try it in a deep pool under the cliffs about a mile above the ranch, and below an old dam, which had originally been built for the purpose of supplying water to an irrigating ditch. I thought the fly too large, but Jim insisted that heavy fish had been caught higher up the river on similar flies, and so I took the first opportunity of trying it in the cliff pool. The result was that halfway down the stream I felt a draw, raised my hand, and the next moment my little cane trout rod was bent double, while a heavy fish, playing like a salmon, ran up and down the pool. I never saw him, and presently the old gut cast parted. But I felt satisfied that this was a considerably heavier fish than anything I had yet hooked.

My next experience of rainbow trout was in the Mississippi Valley. I had been staying for a week on a business visit in the large western town of Minneapolis, situated on the banks of the Mississippi River. A blazing August sun made the dusty streets distinctly unpleasant, raising a thirst that was difficult, although not altogether impossible, to quench, and by contrast brought to my mind longing thoughts of the rippling burns of my native land, some four thousand miles away where grouse were falling, and trout were being caught by my more fortunate countrymen, while I was contracting business and drinking lager beer in the State of Minnesota with the thermometer ninety five degrees in the shade.

I was lunching that day with one of my business friends. Our American cousins are the most hospitable of men. The conversation turned on fishing. With insular prejudice, I openly and most unfavourably contrasted the muddy Mississippi and its catfish and 'Suckers' with the salmon and trout-stocked waters of bonnie Scotland,

'Would you like to catch some rainbow trout?' said my host. 'Where are they?' I doubtingly asked. 'Thirty miles away I can show you plenty,' he answered.

I had three days to spare, and the matter was at once arranged. My incredulity as to the existence of the trout, or indeed of fishable water anywhere within reasonable distance in which to catch them, was, I trust, more or less successfully concealed. The country was dried up with drought. It had not rained for two months, and at

that moment extensive forest fires were raging in the
northern part of the state.

The next afternoon, in company with two grain
men, a judge, and a doctor, we started on our fishing
picnic thirty miles by rail and four by road. In the evening
we found ourselves at our destination, a temperance
country hotel (where, by the by, some of the best bottled
beer in the state was obtainable), kept by a naturalised
German, and situated in the rolling and wooded uplands
of northern Minnesota. At supper, where a dish of fresh
trout finally dispelled my doubts as to their existence,
the situation was more fully explained. Close to the hotel
were at least a dozen natural springs of the clearest water
and of considerable united volume, permanently feeding
a stream that ran for some two miles in alternate rapid
and pool to the river below. At its head this stream was
dammed back into two miniature lakes, where the trout
were every season artificially reared, and thence stocked
the stream for its whole length to where another dam
and pool, with protected outlet, prevented the escape of
the fish to the river below.

Our landlord was a practised fisherman, as I soon
found out; and, moreover, he thoroughly understood
the artificial rearing of trout. He was inclined to look
with contempt on the fishing capabilities of the parties
of town-bred Americans who periodically visited him on
fishing picnics.

The gentle art of fly-fishing is not generally practised
or understood on the banks of the Mississippi. Would

his trout rise to the fly? Certainly they would. What size did they run? Up to three pounds; average half a pound. What flies did they take?

Specimens were shown me of three-quarter-inch flies of a size and shape calculated to put down any well brought up Highland trout for a week. I had a few Scottish flies with me, and produced them. They were not thought much of, and I held my peace. Evidently Minnesota trout had views of their own.

But I had given the impression of expertise and heartily admit that it was a mistake to seem so confident in a place so unfamiliar. My colleagues caught fish the next morning while I was shown up as a complete duffer. First the trout ignored my flies, then my line clunked on to the water, scaring the fish. Then, when all hope was lost, I hooked the grandaddy of them all and while I inwardly heaved a sigh of relief and thought, 'Ah this will show them,' I failed to pay enough attention to the business in hand and, with savage lunge, the trout was gone. No other trout came near me that day. My humiliation was complete.

F. G. Aflalo, *A Book of Fishing Stories,* 1913

Monster Mahseer

THERE WERE the other days on which we came in for great reward, for fish weighing from ten pounds to fifty pounds were quite within the range of moderate expectation, while monsters of far greater weight were known to dwell in the river, and we were ever in hope of hooking one of these.

Many we took out of the Chenab in our time, but never the monster. In the end, however, my regiment held the record with a fish of fifty-two pounds, although we were handsomely beaten in actual best take for a single day, for the commanding officer of another gallant regiment, able to grant himself leave when we could not get away, and never foregoing the privilege, landed one fine day the much-envied score of sixteen fish to his own rod. Great fish they were, too, the total weight of them being nothing less than two hundred pounds. No wonder we found some little difficulty in congratulating him.

Here, too, in the Chenab, the conditions under which we caught our fish were ever a mystery. Water, weather and season would be apparently identical on the days of great success and on those other days with never a fish. Some days we would troll over the same stretch of water time and time again without result. Then, all of a sudden, the fish would come at the bait as if possessed. This was the case on the day that gave me my first forty-pounder. My companion, already into one

that proved almost as heavy, had landed his boat in order
to play his fish, and I, resisting the usual temptation of
offering good advice, essayed to prove my pet theory
that mahseer have a certain moment at which they must
feed, by taking a cast from the shore. The theory held
good in practice for, sure enough, next moment I had
him, and then came a splendid fight. It was a strenuous
dance he led me up and down the bank for thirty-five
glorious if anxious minutes.

Happily, the channel was clear, and there was little
or no danger from rapid or snag, yet, with such a heavy
fish in play, no minute was free from anxiety, and every
mad rush seemed to mark the end. When at last the fish
took to rolling over and over far out in the stream, it
seemed impossible that the gut could bear the strain, and,
as a matter of fact, my misgivings on the subject proved
well-founded, for, as I afterwards discovered, the gut was
actually severed and disaster had been averted only by its
having jammed so tightly between the treble hooks as
to hold the great fish in its final struggles. It was a good
thing that I was spared this knowledge until the fish was
safe on the bank, else I might not have had the courage
to go through with it. Three more, all of them good fish,
we got out of that reach, and the luck was such as to
carry us through many another less successful day. These
were great times no doubt, yet I wonder whether, after
all, the simpler incidents much earlier in my Indian days
were not even happier. There was the far off time, for
instance, when, under the spell of my first introduction

to mahseer, I would gallop out a good nine miles on a hot weather morning, starting at three in the morning so as to be on the water hours before sunrise. The ignoble bait used on these occasions was nothing more than a pellet of dough, and the one pool had to be assiduously groundbaited for days before my visit.

Not a fish would move after the sun was once on the water so the sport had to be short and sharp and it was fun while it lasted, for I never once remember drawing blank.

A few lumps of dough were thrown into the pool on arrival just to attract and locate the fish after which came the cast, a rush from all directions and a fish on the rod its size depending on which first got to the bait.

The madness of the first rush was particularly noticeable here, probably owing to the eagerness of the fish to make good its prize in the presence of so much competition.

Half a dozen would be the usual morning's take and I was able to get back in good time to provide fresh fish for the mess breakfast.

True, these fish never exceeded a weight of from one to five pounds, but even that was satisfactory when contrasted with my previous experience of nothing but small trout at home. In the more sophisticated moods of after years such sport would have seemed too trivial to be thought of, but in those early days it was very welcome.

It was about this period that befell one of those incidents that the fisherman never forgets. I was not actively on a fishing trip, but had been told by an old hand that at a certain spot on the marching road to Cashmere, whither I was bound after ibex, a small stream joined the Jhelum River and that if I were to try a cast or two at the junction, I might reasonably look forward to hooking something monstrous.

The rod was therefore taken along and the expert's instructions obeyed to the letter. A frog was to be the bait and it was indeed about the only sort of bait appropriate to this season of dirty flood water, though I never again fell thus far. At any rate, the result warranted the experiment, for I had not been fishing more than ten minutes when the jerk came and the mahseer was off on its proverbial non-stop rush, fortunately upstream and in the slacker current above the tributary.

I could form no estimate of its size but I knew that I had never felt anything like it before. It was absolutely beyond control, although I could plainly see that if the fish once got out in the mainstream, it would be all over in a moment. Up and down the water it raced, backwards and forwards, with nearly all my line out, alarmingly close to the main current, yet mercifully turning just at the crucial spot, wholly of its own sweet will, for I had no control over its movements whatever. Ten minutes of this followed, and then the fish suddenly determined to go downstream. It showed no sign of tiring and, of course, I was brought up all standing by the tributary stream, too deep to be crossed except by swimming. This was out of the question, as I could never have got across while holding on to the rod with such a fish at the other end. Then it was that my young attendant, whom I had so far overlooked, had an inspiration.

'Give me the rod, Sahib,' he said. 'I can easily take it over, while you run round by the bridge.'

This suggested a happy solution of the difficulty and, after warning the youngster to hold on like grim death, I raced for the bridge. The young fellow swam like a duck and the mahseer behaved just as I could have wished. Feeling it once again at the end of the rod, when I took back the rod, I all but laughed aloud in the certainty of success. Alas!

Whether its anger had been roused by the unavoidable jerking of the rod during the swim, or whether it simply judged the time had come to put an end to such fooling and get down to business, the grim fact remains that, within a few moments of my recovering the rod, the fish dashed off downstream and out into the middle of the stream. No check was possible, and, as the mahseer lurched and struggled, borne down by the irresistible current, I got one unforgettable glimpse of its vast proportions. I rushed madly down the bank, helplessly watching the line disappear off the reel until it was all out. Then came one final pull, and the fish of my life was gone.

Here, then, although it ended in dismal failure, was the greatest moment in all my memories of mahseer. Yet, as has been said, it was but one of many memorable fishing episodes, and it would be hard to say whether, if there is any comparison between the two, it really gave me more excitement than that remote triumph when, as a boy, I successfully landed an enormous half-pound trout while the other boy, more mindful of home instructions, dutifully paused to remove his boots.

F. G. Aflalo, *A Book of Fishing Stories,* 1913

Chapter 3

MAKING
MISCHIEF

Conger Attack

IN NO SPORT is the glorious uncertainty more in
evidence than in sea fishing – it is not so much what we
do catch as what we may catch. In freshwater the roach
fisher catches roach, the bream fisher bream, and so on.
We know our limit. But in the sea, here indeed is possibility
unlimited; what will the next minute bring us? Who knows.
It may be the humblest rockfish, it may be the mighty
conger, it may be – there is nothing it may not be.

Lying lazily at anchor some two miles out in the
bay, lulled by the gentle lapping of the sun-kissed
wavelets, fanned by a summer breeze that brings with

it all the purity and freshness of the Atlantic, his must be a sorry heart indeed that cannot feel the joy of such surroundings. You are just thinking – sport for the nonce being quiet – that a few minutes in dreamland would not be amiss, when, suddenly, 'Hi,' shouts the boatman, 'Hi. Your rod, sir.' The word 'rod' wakes you, and none too soon, for there it is bending to the water as do the rushes in a gale of wind.

'He's on! He's on!' you cry, as you seize your rod, and by Jove we're off.

'Let that cable slip man, cut it,' you call to the skipper, who is lazily preparing to haul the anchor. 'Let it go man, he's taken nearly all my line, I can't hold him I tell you. Let it go!' Oh, the wild excitement of that moment; another second and it seems he must break you but the skipper sees this is no time for slowly hauling cables – a half-hitch around a spar and over goes the line and we are free; free to follow wherever this veritable King of the Deeps may choose to lead us.

It is not that he tows us – my line would not stand that – but he is heading away from the boat, and we must humour this first wild rush or lose him. The skipper has the oars out now and is standing up to it, watching my every movement in the bow – no need to give him instructions.

He, myself and the rod are fighting as one man – it is three to one, and yet the fish still holds his own. Every second brings some fresh excitement; my footing is none too firm.

'Take care, sir, take care,' he says as I step on a rope and lurch seawards, and the occasion calls for care – I feel it, I know it; a false move, a little too much strain, a moment's slack and there will be nothing left us but to reel in some hundred yards of plaited hemp and to reel out some – well every fisherman knows what to reel out on an occasion like that.

The strain is lessening now, 'Back her,' I cry. 'Alright, sir, I know.' says the skipper a little crossly, 'you leave that to me, sir.'

'Sorry,' I answer, and he gives me a nod and a mollified grunt. But all my attention is wanted for the rod again, he is now bucking, positively bucking, as a smack does when it crosses the harbour bar and hits the rough seas, she seems to stop dead and buck, and so it was with my fish.

'What can it be,' I say softly to the skipper. 'Lord knows,' he answers back in the same tone.

This is no time for shouting and excitement, there is headwork to be done and we must keep cool. We get a rest now for a few moments – the fish is sulking – and I have time to get a better footing, then suddenly he is off again. Nothing is said, and save for the creaking of the oars, and an occasional turn of the reel, the fight goes on in silence. But we are winning, the distance between decreases – slowly the line is coming back to me, every inch of it well fought though.

'Ah,' says the skipper softly. 'Ah,' say I, and then together we cry 'conger' – only a glimpse of him though, and then down he goes straight. He is enormous.

'Are we on rock,' I shout excitedly.

'Sand, only sand, not so much as pebble down there,' he answers, and I sigh, relieved.

The end is close at hand now, the skipper has put by the oars, and I see him quietly fitting up the gaff and watching the spot where my line cuts the water; it will be his turn soon. A few more turns of the reel, and then – then a mighty boil in the water, a moment's awful suspense, a flash of steel, and seven feet of writhing furious conger is roaming up and down our boat seeking whom he may devour; the excitement is not over yet, it is one thing to get a conger in the boat and another to keep him there – thwack, goes an oar, and snap goes his mouth as he closes on a rope – it is our chance, he is still a moment, thwack goes the oar again – but we miss and the mighty eel makes a huge bound, sinks his teeth into the skipper's leg. A mighty roar, we beat the conger down but the skipper has lurched against the gunnel and as we loosen the conger's teeth with blows he somehow manages to thrash his way over the side and in an instant he is gone. All that is left to us is a gashed leg and a deep sense of disappointment. That is one conger who will not so easily be caught again.

Robert Stanley, *Angling Anecdotes,* 1903

Lost Beneath the Lilies

IN THE WEST; on the east, within a hundred yards under a slope, is Lough Beg. We find the perfect bay but most of the shore is defended against the angler by a wide expanse of water lilies, with their pretty white floating lamps, or by tall sedges and reeds. One short sloping shingle beach allows access. Nor is the wading easy. Four steps you make with safety, at the fifth your foremost leg sinks in mud apparently bottomless. Most people fish only the eastern side, whereof a few score yards are open, with a rocky and gravelly bottom.

Now, all loughs have their humours. In some, trout like a big fly, in some a small one, but almost all do best with a rough wind or rain. I knew enough of Lough Beg to approach it at noon on a blazing day of sunshine, when the surface was like glass. It was like that when first I saw it and a shepherd warned us that we would do nothing; we did little, indeed, but I rose nearly every rising fish I cast over, losing them all, and in some cases being broken, as I was using very fine gut, and the fish were heavy.

Another trial seemed desirable, and the number of rising trout was most tempting.

All over the lough trout were rising to the natural fly, with big circles like those you see in the Test at twilight; while in the centre, where no artificial fly can be cast for want of a boat, a big fish would throw himself out of the water in his eagerness. One such I saw that could not have weighed under three pounds, a short, thick, dark yellow fish.

I was using a light two-handed rod, and fancied that a single Test fly on very fine tackle would be the best lure. It certainly rose the trout, if one threw into the circle they made; but they never were hooked.

One fish of about a pound and a half threw himself out of the water at my fly, hit it, and broke the fine tackle. So I went on raising them, but never getting them. As long as the sun blazed and no breeze ruffled the water, they rose bravely, but a cloud or even a ripple seemed to send them down.

At last I tried a big alder, and with that I actually touched a few, and even landed several on the shelving bank. Their average weight, as we proved on several occasions, was exactly three-quarters of a pound, but we never succeeded in landing any of the really big ones.

A local angler told me he had caught one of two pounds and had another 'like a young grilse' after he had drawn it on to the bank.

I can easily believe it for in no lough but one have I ever seen so many really big and handsome fish feeding. Lough Beg is within a mile of a larger and more famous loch, but it is infinitely better, although the other looks much more favourable in all ways for sport.

The only place where fishing is easy, as I have said, is a narrow strip of coast under the hill where there is some shingle and the mouth of a very tiny feeder stream,

usually dry. Off this place the trout rise freely but never
so freely as in a certain corner, quite out of reach without
a boat where the leviathans lived and sported.

After the little expanse of open shore had been
fished over a few times, the trout there seemed to grow
more shy and there was a certain monotony in walking
this tiny quarter-deck of space, so I went around to the
west side where the water lilies are.

Fish were rising about ten yards beyond the weedy
beds, and I foolishly thought I would try for them. Now,
you cannot overestimate the difficulty of casting a fly
across yards of water lilies. You catch in the weeds as
you lift your line for a fresh cast, and then you have to
extricate it laboriously, shortening line, and then to let it
out again, and probably come to grief once more.

I saw a heavy trout rise, with a huge sullen circle
dimpling around him, cast over him, raised him, and
missed him. The water was perfectly still, and the plop
made by these fish was very exciting and tantalising.

The next that rose took the alder, and, of course,
ran right into the broad band of lilies. I tried all the
dodges I could think of, and all that Mr Halford suggests.
I dragged at him hard. I gave him line. I sat down and
endeavoured to disengage my thoughts, but I never got
a glimpse of him, and finally had to wade as far in as I
dared and save as much of the casting line as I could, and
it was very little.

There was one thing to be said for the trout on this
side: they meant business. They did not rise shyly, like the

others, but went for the fly if it came at all near them, and then down they rushed, and bolted into the lily roots.

A new plan occurred to me. I put on about eighteen inches of the stoutest gut I had, to the end I knotted the biggest sea trout fly I possessed and, hooking the next fish that rose, I turned my back on the lough and ran uphill with the rod. Looking back, I saw a trout well over a pound flying across the lilies; but alas, the hold was not strong enough, and he fell back. Again and again I tried this method, invariably hooking the trout, though the heavy, short casting line and the big fly fell very awkwardly in the dead stillness of the water. I had some exciting runs with them, for they came eagerly to the big fly, and did not miss it, as they had missed the Red Quill, or Whitchurch Dun, with which at first I tried to beguile them. One, of only the average weight, did drag out over the lilies; the others fell off mid-journey, but they never broke the uncompromisingly taut tackle.

With the first chill of evening they ceased rising. Very peculiar. The chances are that the trout beyond the band of weeds never see an artificial fly, and they are, therefore, the more guileless – at least, late in the season. In spring, I believe, the lilies are less in the way, and I fear someone has put a steam boat on the lough in April. But it is not so much what one catches in Lough Beg, as the monsters that one might catch that makes the tarn so desirable. The lough seems to prove that any hill tarn might be made a good place for sport, if trout were introduced where they do not exist already. But the size of these in Lough Beg puzzles me, nor can one see how they breed, as breed they do for twice or thrice I caught a fingerling and threw him in again.

But the day came when a great dark yellow trout took my fly and then I knew the vast folly of fishing over those lilies. The instant I hooked him he bore powerfully away from the disastrous snags towards the middle of the lough and for a moment I had hopes some miracle might occur and I might land him, but then he turned, leapt once in all his magnificence and then tore towards those tangled roots. I could not turn my winch hard enough to keep pace with him. I knew he was lost long before he was lost. He reached the lilies easily and within seconds my line locked around some deeply sunken, tough old root and he was gone.

Andrew Lang, Angling Sketches, 1891

Death at the Trows

I SHALL never forget the shock with which I read in the *Scotsman*, under Angling, the following paragraph: Tweed – Strange Death of an Angler – An unfortunate event has cast a gloom over fishers in this district. As Mr R. the keeper on the B … Water, was busy angling yesterday, his attention was caught by some object floating on the stream. He cast his flies over it, and landed a soft felt hat,

the ribbon stuck all over with salmon flies, N
hurried upstream with the most lively app.
These were soon justified. In a shallow, below tl
deep and dangerous rapids called The Trows M.
a salmon leaping in a very curious manner. On a
examination, he found that fish was attached to a
About seventy yards higher he found, in shallow wa
the body of a man, the hand still grasping in death tl
butt of the rod, to which the salmon was fast, all the line
being run out.

Mr K. at once rushed into the stream, and dragged
out the body, in which he recognised with horror the
Hon. Houghton Grannon, to whom the water was lately
let. Life had been for some minutes extinct, and though
Mr K. instantly hurried for a doctor, that gentleman
could only attest the melancholy fact.

The wading in The Trows is extremely dangerous
and difficult, and Mr Grannon, who was fond of fishing
without an attendant, must have lost his balance, slipped,
and been dragged down by the weight of his waders.

Andrew Lang, *Angling Sketches,* 1891

Fishing Not Marrying

THE DAY before my wedding day had been the
happiest in my life. Never had I felt so certain of Olive's

affections, never so fortunate in my own. We parted in the soft moonlight, she no doubt to finish her nuptial preparations; I, to seek my couch in the little rural inn above the roaring waters of the river.

> *Move eastward, happy earth, and leave*
> *Yon orange sunset fading slow:*
> *From fringes of the faded eve*
> *Oh, happy planet, eastward go,*

I murmured, though the atmospheric conditions were not really those described by the poet.

> *Ah, bear me with thee, smoothly borne,*
> *Dip forward under starry light,*
> *And move me to my marriage morn,*
> *And round again to …*

I was interrupted.

'River in grand order, sir,' said the voice of Robins, the keeper, who recognised me in the moonlight, 'There's a regular monster in the Ashweil,' he added, naming a favourite cast.

'Never saw nor heard of such a fish in the water before.'

'Dick must catch him, Robins,' I answered, 'No fishing for me tomorrow.'

'No sir,' said Robins, affably. 'Wish you joy, sir, and Miss Olive, too. It's a pity, though! Master Dick, he throws a fine fly, but he gets flurried with a big fish, being young. And this one is a topper.'

With that he gave me good-night, and I went to bed, but not to sleep. I was fevered with happiness, the past and future reeled before my wakeful vision. I heard every clock strike; the sounds of morning were astir, and still I could not sleep.

The ceremony, for reasons connected with our long journey to my father's place in Hampshire, was to be early – half-past ten was the hour. I looked at my watch; it was seven of the clock, and then I looked out of the window: it was a fine, soft grey morning, with a south wind tossing the yellowing boughs. I got up, dressed in a hasty way, and thought I would just take a look at the river. It was, indeed, in glorious order, lapping over the top of the sharp stone that we regarded as a measure of the due size of water.

The morning was young, sleep was out of the question: I could not settle my mind to read. Why should I not take a farewell cast, alone, of course? I always disliked the attendance of a gillie. I took my salmon rod out of its case, rigged it up and started for the stream, which flowed within a couple of hundred yards of my quarters. There it raced under the ash tree, a pale delicate brown, perhaps a little thing too coloured. I therefore put on a large Silver Doctor, and began steadily fishing down the Ash Tree cast.

What if I should wipe Dick's eye, I thought, when just where the rough and smooth water meet there boiled up a head and shoulders such as I had never seen on any fish. My heart leaped and stood still, but there came no sensation from my rod, and I finished the cast, my knees trembling beneath me.

Then I gently lifted the line, and very elaborately tested every link of the powerful casting line. Then I gave him ten minutes by my watch; next, with unspeakable emotion, I stepped into the stream and repeated the cast.

Just at the same spot he came up again: the huge rod bent like a switch, and the salmon rushed straight down the pool, as if he meant to make for the sea; I staggered on to dry land to follow him and dragged at my watch to time the fish; a quarter to eight.

But the slim chain had broken, and the watch, as I hastily thrust it back, missed my pocket and fell into the water. There was no time to stoop for it; the fish started afresh, tore up the pool as fast as he had gone down it, and, rushing behind the torrent, into the eddy at the top, leaped clean out of the water. He was massive, at least forty pounds.

Here he slackened a little, dropping back, and I got in some line. Now he sulked so intensely that I thought he had got the line around a rock. It might be broken, might be holding fast to a sunken stone, for aught that I could tell; and the time was passing, I knew not how rapidly. I tried all known methods, tugging at him, tapping the butt, and slackening line on him. At last the top of the rod was slightly agitated and then back flew the long line in my face and I reeled in with sigh. Gone!

But the line tightened again. He had made a sudden rush under my bank, but there he lay again like a stone. How long? Ah, I cannot tell how long! I heard the church clock strike but missed the number of the strokes.

Soon he started again downstream into the shallows – leaping at the end of his rush – the monster. Then he came slowly up, and jiggered vaguely at the line. It seemed impossible that any tackle could stand these short violent jerks. Soon he showed signs of weakening. Once his huge silver side appeared for a moment near the surface, but he retreated to his old fastness. I was in a tremor of delight and despair. I should have thrown down my rod, and flown on the wings of love to Olive and the altar. But I hoped that there was time still; that it was not so very late.

At length he was failing. I heard ten o'clock strike. He came up and lumbered on the surface of the pool.

Gradually I drew him, plunging ponderously, to the gravelled beach, where I meant to tail him. He yielded to the strain, he was in the shallows. The line was shortened. I stooped to seize him. The frayed and overworn gut broke at the knot and he rolled forever back into the deep.

I leaped after him, but he slipped from my arms. In that moment I knew more than the anguish of Orpheus. Orpheus! Had I too lost my Eurydice? I rushed from the stream, up the steep bank, along to my rooms. I passed the church door. Olive, pale as her orange blossoms, was issuing from the porch. The clock pointed to 10.45. I was ruined, I knew it, and I laughed. I laughed like a lost spirit. She swept past me, and, amidst the amazement of the gentle and simple, I sped wildly away. Ask me no more. The rest is silence.

Andrew Lang, *Angling Sketches,* 1891

Tyne Wave

AN EXTRAORDINARY accident occurred on the River Tyne last week.

Mr Billings from Wylam was fishing the river for salmon near Hexham when a great wave – like the Severn bore said one witness – came up the river and toppled the poor fisherman into deep water. Mr Billings had been wading, which no doubt contributed to the ease with which he was unbalanced.

Before anyone could offer assistance he had been swept downstream. It took only a few minutes for the alarm to be raised but too late for Mr Billing, whose lifeless body was found by a boatman an hour after the incident.

The mystery of what caused the wave, estimated at between eighteen inches and two feet in height, has not been solved.

Hexham Courant, April 1878

Pike Escape

THE WORST of it is, that good pike waters are very hard of access nowadays. As a general rule they are strictly preserved, and where they are not so, are over-fished and poached, so that they are scarcely worth a visit. Very often the best sport is to be had in deep pools in trout rivers, where the pike has made his home unnoticed, and where nobody thinks of fishing for him.

In spite of a commandment against envying one's neighbour's possessions, I always envy the man who has a good pike pool or river all to himself and his friends. For him there is no asking for leave and incurring an obligation. He can go when he pleases and have his fill of sport without having to ask any man for permission. The summit of my angling ambition is to possess a pike pool, or a right of fishing in one when I please. Now that I have made my wants known, perhaps some kind friend will step forward and give me that which I have pike-fished in many waters, and have caught my fair share of pike, but up to the time of which I write I had never caught any really large fish. I had caught plenty of good-sized ones, up to ten or twelve pounds or so, but none of your monster fish of thirty, forty, and fifty pounds in weight. I had seen a friend catch one of thirty-three pounds in weight, and that was the nearest I had ever been to a big fish. Many a time I had gone to noted pike waters expecting to do wonders and building very pleasing castles in the air, but the same confounded mediocrity always attended my best efforts.

I was on a visit some little time ago in one of the western counties and in the course of a picnic excursion we came upon a lake embosomed in woods that at once took my fancy as the very beau ideal of a pike pool. It was surrounded with reeds and rushes, its shores curved in many a quiet bay margined with lilies where the coot and the moorhen swam with a tameness and sense of security that showed that they were not often disturbed. A light breeze was rippling the pool, and every now and then a rush of small fish out of the pool showed where the pike were chasing them. The remembrance of that pool quite haunted me for a long time to come, and the desire to fish in it was fanned by the tales that our host told me of the wondrously large pike to be caught there. It was strictly preserved, and very seldom fished.

Sometime afterwards I accidentally made the acquaintance of its owner. We became good friends – for the possession of this pike pool made him seem a very pleasant fellow in my eyes. I cunningly led him up to the subject of fishing, and to his pike pool, and the end of it was that he invited me to spend a short time with him at his house, and to help to catch some of its large pike; for he was an angler only his tastes ran upon salmon fishing and nothing pleased him better than going to Norway.

A clear, dry frosty night in January saw me with my legs under my friend's mahogany. We were to fish the Mere on the morrow, and everything was prepared for our sport. The gamekeeper had obtained a quantity of gudgeon from a neighbouring river, and they had been kept fresh and lively in a tank sunk in the Mere. Ere the coffee came in I had heard many wonderful stories about the immense fish that were to be caught in the Mere, and went to bed perfectly convinced that at last I was to realise my dreams, and catch some monster pike; and I slept uneasily.

We were up and about on our way to the lake. It was a brilliantly bright morning – so dry and frosty that the stiff north-east wind blew golden clouds of dust along the roads. The sun, as he climbed over the oak plantation, threw his level beams across the undulating meadows, which were barred with steps of deep, dark, and brilliant light green, as they lay in sunlight or shadow.

We lost little time in embarking, and, selecting good-sized gudgeons; we baited our spinning tackle and proceeded to trail our baits around the Mere. The wavelets leaped cheerily against the side of our boat, and the water fowl swam lazily before us or flew into the rustling reeds. The sheltered corners of the bays were coated with ice. The reeds were laid and rotted by the frost; the water was just the right colour and it seemed a perfect day both for enjoyment and for sport. Our expectations were high, and it seemed as if they were to be realised.

In the first round we caught six pike but what rather astonished me was that they were all under five pounds in weight. We were halfway round a second time, just off the mouth of a weedy bay, when my rod gave a great lunge, and was nearly torn out of my hand. I struck, and it was evident that I was fast into a mighty fish.

'Keep him away from the weeds,' exclaimed my companion, 'You have caught a whopper, and no mistake.'

There was no need for his caution to keep the fish away from the weeds. The pike made straight for the centre of the Mere, running out my line at a fearful rate. I let go the line grudgingly, for I expected him to make a dash back for the weeds, when my line would be doubled up and I should lose my fish. But the pike had no such intention. He went straight ahead, without pause in his steady rush, until my line, which was eighty yards long, was nearly all out. I gave him the butt and held on until I thought my rod would have broken in the hope of turning him, but he still went on, and then, as my rod was staunch and my line was strong, our boat began to move after the pike.

'By Jove! This is wonderful,' said my friend. 'You have hooked a leviathan. Play him steadily and skilfully, and don't get excited.'

Now that was very good advice if it could be carried out, but as the speaker was already white and trembling with excitement, and I was, if anything, worse, his advice was not of much use. Well, I stood in the bows of the boat, and the monster towed us with increasing swiftness right across the lake, which was about a quarter of a mile broad at this part. When we came to the weeds at the other side of the Mere he turned back again, and to prevent undue strain on the rod in turning the boat, I ran to the other end of it, and we were towed back again in precisely the same way, and at a fair three miles an hour pace. Our excitement was fast turning to awe when, on reaching the other side of the mere, the brute turned again and began to make a slow detour of the lake, stopping every now and then to sulk at the bottom, but never allowing us to get back much of our line, or to catch a glimpse of him. In this way long minutes passed, and the case began to assume a serious aspect.

'Don't get into a funk, old man. I have seen salmon take very much longer to land; and I have heard of one being on nineteen hours at a stretch, and when he was caught he was not a very big one, either.'

'Aye, that is all very well for a salmon, but a pike does not fight so long. I saw a thirty-three pounder landed in a quarter of an hour, so this must be a veritable shark.'

Well, matters went on in this way until four hours had elapsed, and still we seemed no nearer to the end.

Then, seventy yards away there was a huge boil at the top of the water, and the strain on the rod slackened.

'Hurrah! There he is. He is beginning to give in. It will only be a short time now.' My friend was right. Little by little I wound in my line, and nearer and nearer the monster came. At last we could distinctly see him rushing and wallowing about with widely distended mouth, in the clear water. In length he was about five feet, and his weight, it is clear, must have been fifty pounds. What a proud man I felt at that moment. All my hopes were on the point of being realised. I drew him slowly and carefully in, and my friend got the net ready. And then without a wrench or a struggle or indeed any further movement from the mighty fish, the line broke and my record fish was gone with a flick of the tail.

George Davies, *Angling Idylls,* 1876

Chapter 4

A Little Local Difficulty

Abandoned by the Goddess of Fishing

IT WAS about the first day of October, and we had enjoyed a spate. Salmon fishing is a mere child of the weather; with rain almost anybody may raise fish, without it all art is apt to be vain. We had been blessed with a spate. On Wednesday the Tweed had been roaring red from bank to bank.

Salmon fishing was wholly out of the question, and it is to be feared that the innumerable trout fishers, busy on every eddy, were baiting with salmon roe – an illegal lure. On Thursday the red tinge had died out of the water, but only a very strong wader would have ventured in; others had a good chance, if they tried it, of being picked up at Berwick.

Friday was the luckless day of my own failure and broken heart. The water was still very heavy and turbid, a frantic wind was lashing the woods, heaps of dead leaves floated down and several sheaves of corn were drifted on the current. The longboat pool at Yair, however, is sheltered by wooded banks, and it was possible enough to cast, in spite of the wind's fury. We had driven from a place about five miles distant, and we had not driven three hundred yards before I remembered that we had forgotten the landing net. But, as I expected nothing, it did not seem worthwhile to go back for this indispensable implement.

We reached the waterside, and found that the trout were feeding below the pendent branches of the trees and in the quiet, deep eddies of the long boat pool. One cannot see rising trout without casting over them, in preference to labouring after salmon, so I put up a small rod and diverted myself from the bank. It was to little purpose. Tweed trout are now grown very shy and capricious; even a dry fly failed to do any execution worth mentioning. Conscience compelled me, as I had been sent out by kind hosts to fish for salmon, not to neglect my orders. The armour – the ponderous gear of the fisher – was put on with the enormous boots, and the gigantic rod was equipped. Then came the beginning of sorrows. We had left the books of salmon flies comfortably reposing at home. We had also forgotten the whisky flask. Everything, in fact, except cigarettes had been left behind. Unluckily, not quite everything: I had a trout fly book, and therein lay just one large salmon fly. Not a Tweed fly but a lure that is used on the beautiful and hopeless waters of the distant Ken, in Galloway.

It had brown wings, a dark body and a piece of jungle cock feather, and it was fastened to a sea trout casting line. Now, if I had possessed no salmon flies at all, I must either have sent back for some or gone on innocently dallying with trout. But this one wretched fly lured me to my ruin. I saw that the casting line had a link that seemed rather twisted. I tried it, but, in the spirit of Don Quixote with his helmet, I did not try it hard. I waded into the easiest looking part of the pool, just above a huge tree that dropped its boughs to the water, and began casting, merely from a sense of duty.

I had not cast a dozen times before there was a heavy, slow plunge in the stream, and a glimpse of purple and azure.

'That's him,' cried a man who was trouting on the opposite bank. Doubtless it was 'him', but he had not touched the hook. I believe the correct thing would have been to wait for half an hour, and then try the fish with a smaller fly. But I had no smaller fly – no other fly at all.

I stepped back a few paces and fished down again. In Major Traherne's work I have read that the heart leaps, stands still, or otherwise betrays an uncomfortable interest when one casts for the second time over a salmon that has risen. I cannot honestly say that I suffered from this tumultuous emotion.

'He will not come again,' I said, when there was a long, heavy drag at the line, followed by a shrieking of the reel, as in Mr William Black's novels. Let it be confessed that the first hooking of a salmon is an excitement unparalleled in trout fishing. There have been anglers who, when the salmon was once on, handed him over to the gillie to play and land. One would like to act as gillie to those lordly amateurs. My own fish rushed downstream, where the big tree stands. I had no hope of landing him if he took that course, because one could neither pass the rod under the boughs nor wade out beyond them. But he soon came back, while one took in line and discussed his probable size with the trout fisher opposite. His size, indeed! Nobody knows what it was, for when he had come up to the point whence he had started he began a policy of violent short tugs – not jiggering, as it is called, but plunging with all his weight on the line. I had clean forgotten the slimness of the tackle and, as he was clearly well hooked, held him perhaps too hard. Only a very raw beginner likes to take hours over landing a fish. Perhaps I held him too tight; at all events, after a furious plunge, back came the line, the casting line had snapped at the top link. A terrible disaster and all brought on me by my own stupidity.

There was no more to be said or done, except to hunt for another fly in the trout fly book. Here there was no such thing, but a local spectator offered me a huge fly, more like a gaff, and equipped with a large iron eye for attaching the gut. Withal I suspect this weapon was meant, not for fair fishing, but for sniggling. Now sniggling is a form of cold-blooded poaching. In the open water, on the Ettrick, you may see half a dozen snigglers busy. They all wear high wading trousers; they are all armed with stiff salmon rods and huge flies. They push the line and the top joints of the rod deep into the water, drag it along, and then bring the hook out with a jerk. Often it sticks in the side of a salmon, and in this most unfair and unsportsmanlike way the free sport of honest people is ruined and fish are diminished in number.

Now, the big fly may have been an honest character, but he was sadly like a rake hook in disguise. He did not look as if any fish could fancy him. I therefore sent a messenger across the river to beg, buy, or borrow a fly at The Nest. But this pretty cottage is no longer the home of the famous angling club, which has gone a mile or two up the water and builded for itself a new dwelling. My messenger came back with one small fatigued looking fly: a Popham, I think, which had been lent by someone at a farmhouse.

The water was so heavy that the small fly seemed useless; however, we fastened it on as a dropper, using the sniggler as the trail fly; so exhausted were our resources that I had to cut a piece of gut off a minnow tackle and attach the small fly to that.

The tiny gut loop of the fly was dreadfully frayed, and with a heavy heart I began fishing again. My friend on the opposite side called out that big fish were rising in the bend of the stream, so thither I went, stumbling over rocks, and casting with much difficulty, as the high overgrown banks permit no backward sweep of the line.

You are obliged to cast by a kind of forward thrust of the arms, a knack not to be acquired in a moment. I splashed away awkwardly, but at last managed to make a straight, clean cast. There was a slight pull, such as a trout gives in mid-stream under water. I raised the point, and again the reel sang aloud and gleefully as the salmon rushed down the stream farther and faster than the first.

It is a very pleasant thing to hook a salmon when you are all alone, as I was then – alone with yourself and the Goddess of Fishing. This salmon, just like the other, now came back, and instantly began the old tactics of heavy plunging tugs. But I knew the gut was sound this time, and as I fancied he had risen to the sniggler, had no anxiety about the tackle holding. One more plunge, and back came the line as before. He was off. I wanted to weep. One could have sat down and gnawed at the reel. What had gone wrong? Why, the brute had taken the old fly from the farmhouse and had snapped the loop that attaches the gut. The little loop was still on the fragment of minnow tackle that fastened it to the cast. There was no more chance, for there were now no more flies, except a small 'cobbery', a sea trout fly from the Sound of Mull. It was time for us to go, with a heavy heart and a basket empty, except for two or three miserable trout. The loss of the salmon was not the whole misfortune. All the chances of the day were gone, and seldom have salmon risen so freely.

I had not been casting long enough to smoke half a cigarette when I hooked that fish. The salmon were rising at flies which were the exact opposites of each other in size, character, and colour. They were ready to rise at anything but the sniggler. And I had nothing to offer them – absolutely nothing bigger than a small red-spinner from the Test. On that day a fisher, not far off, hooked nine salmon and landed four of them, in one pool. Never had such a chance come before and never was it to come again for me.

Next day I fished again in the same water with a friend. I rose a fish, but did not hook it and he landed a small one five minutes after we started and we only had one other rise all the rest of the day. Probably it was not dark and windy enough, but who can explain the caprices of salmon? The only certain thing is, that carelessness brings misfortune; that if your tackle is weak fish will hook themselves on days and in parts of the water where you expected nothing, and then will go away with your fly and your casting lines. Fortune never forgives. He who is lazy, and takes no trouble because he expects no fish, will always be meeting heart-breaking adventures. One should never make a hopeless or careless cast; bad luck lies in wait for that kind of performance. These are the experiences that embitter a man, as they embittered

Dean Swift, who, old and ill, neglected and in Irish exile, still felt the pang of losing a great trout when he was a boy; what pleasure is there in such landscapes and tradition if such accidents befall you?

J. H. Vahey, *The Humane Angler,* 1910

That Old Line!

OF LINES it is only necessary to say that tapered waterproof plaited silk lines are excellent, but I think, at any rate for trout fishing, that nothing is better than a Manchester waterproof plaited cotton line; when it is new it goes into the eye of the wind beautifully. I think the silk line is better than the other after each has had a season's wear, but although lines, if carefully and regularly dried, will last a long time, they should be tested frequently and not trusted too long.

A ludicrous accident once happened to me, when fishing for salmon with an old line. It was a pouring wet morning, and just at the critical moment when the river began to rise I hooked a salmon in a broad open stretch of water. This salmon played sulkily; after a few minutes I tried to reel in some line, but the fish was not very willing; the wet line would not run easily on the dripping rod, and broke suddenly about halfway up the rod. I was alone, but the fish, not understanding the situation, gave

me time to lay down the rod, and knot the line rapidly
to a ring. What I ought to have done, of course, was to
join the two ends of line near the reel, and trust to being
able to play the fish without needing more line than was
already out: had I done this I should have retained for
myself the privilege of being able to reel in line. But
to do this would have taken longer, the fish might have
made a bolt while I was doing it, and I was in great terror
and had no time to reflect. The result was that when
communications were re-established, I was attached to
a salmon about twenty yards away, without any power
either of reducing the distance, or of allowing it to be
increased.

Far below me was a broad extent of shingle, and
I fought to gain this. The river was at least forty yards
broad, but the salmon kindly restricted all his struggles
to my side, and at last I stood upon the shingle, on a level
with the water, and with flat ground on which I could
retire from the water's edge. This I began to do, and was
succeeding yard by yard when the hold gave and the fly
came back to me. Then followed the thought of how
much better things might have been managed, and the
blank despair of knowing that with a rapidly rising river,
there was no chance of another salmon that day.

On one other occasion my reel line broke. I had
hooked a salmon, which ran up into some water full of
notorious sunken rocks, among which the line got fast. I
put on a strain in every possible direction, and tried pulling
by hand, but could move nothing and feel nothing. As a

last resort, I let out all my line and went down to the full length of it in order to get a pull as directly downstream as possible. The line broke unexpectedly, close to the reel, and in a moment was swept out of the rings by the stream, and into the river, and I saw it no more that day. But the next morning my friend, wading on the opposite side in slack water, felt something around his feet, and at luncheon presented me with the whole of the lost line and part of the cast still attached to it. The fish, of course, was long gone.

Edward Grey, Fly Fishing, 1907

Mud in Your Eye

ONE DAY I was going to fish Captain S's water on the Wylye and on walking up the river past what we used to call Horse Pool, where there was a lot of iris growing, the bank of the river being very soft and swampy, I saw a very large trout move out of a little muddy bay, which was surrounded by those iris, into the river. I made up my mind to look out for him in the evening.

When I came to the place at about 6.30 I approached very carefully and put a fly over the iris into the little bay. The fly was at once taken and the trout rushed out into the river. He did not fight much, but soon gave in. But he was a very big fish. I had with me a net, the handle of

which was jointed in the middle and when it was opened
out it had a reach of some five feet. I approached the
river very, very carefully, bending down the irises so as
to walk on them, and at last I got the trout into the net.

I was just congratulating myself, as it was the
biggest trout I had ever hooked in the river, when, alas,
all at once without any warning the ground gave way,
and I sank into the black mud almost to my waist. I must
confess that I lost my head, for if I had only turned the
net over, all would have been well; but as it was the net
went into the water and the trout swam out, and while I
was getting out of the mud the fish, the best I was ever
to hook in that river, broke me and was gone.

John Buckland, *Logbook of a Fisherman*, 1876

The Road to Hell ...

SOME FORTY years ago several thousands of Loch
Leven trout were put into the Wylye. For a few years these
fish gave most excellent sport; they were very free risers
and, when hooked, fought well, and they were beautiful
looking fish. Everyone said how they had improved the
fishing and how much better they were than the old
Wylye trout.

Then, rather suddenly, came a season when the
fishing fell off very much indeed; there seemed to

be a scarcity of fish, especially the smaller ones. On investigation it was found that these Loch Levens, which had by now become big fish, had left the shallows and had got into the deep mill holes, where they had turned cannibal and were little better than pike. They had developed enormous heads, and had mouths large enough to swallow a half-pound fish of any kind. This caused endless trouble for a time, as all these deep holes had to be netted to get them out, which was no easy matter.

I myself caught one in a deep hole in a ditch with a landing net – a most hideous brute of about three and a half pounds, but there were some caught a good deal bigger than that. The water had to be restocked and it was a number of years before the fishing became even reasonably good again. A fine example of the road to hell being via good intentions.

Langford Brown, *By the Water's Side,* 1936

Down a Hole

WHEN I was at Oxford, I was in the Examination Schools one June, and after I had finished my paperwork I had two days to stay up before my viva. On one of these days I intended to fish. Accordingly, I packed a toothbrush and very little besides, and started off by an early train to fish the Colne at Fairford, to stay the night there and return about the middle of the next day.

When I reached Fairford I found that the mayfly was up. So I bought some at a tackle shop there and started to fish. Almost at once I found a trout of about two pounds greedily feeding on the mayflies that were thick on the river; he was lying in a channel between two large patches of weed. I waded into the river, which was about eighteen inches deep so it only came up to my knees, and got well behind the fish.

He took me at once, and when I started to walk ashore I put my foot on one of the weed patches and at once into a deep hole in the middle of the river, right up to my chest. It was a miracle I wasn't drowned for it was a very deep hole. I lost the fish, spoilt my lunch, which was in my fishing basket, and wetted all my tobacco and my matches.

However, I started to fish again hoping that I would quickly dry out in the hot sun. But this was not to be for within half an hour a thunderstorm came on, with torrents of rain, and as I had no raincoat with me in about two minutes the only dry part of my clothing was as wet as the rest of me. This entirely completed my disaster and there was nothing for it, as the river began to get thick, but to return to the Bull Hotel and go to bed while they dried my clothes in the kitchen. So much for trout fishing during Schools.

Langford Brown, *By the Water's Side*, 1936

Vicar on the Run

THERE USED to be a large sallow bush overhanging the river, growing out of this garden, and if there were any fish in the river at all there was always one under this bush.

It was a horrible, almost impossible place to put a fly, and the stream of the water was all wrong to make the fly work. I do not think that anyone ever landed a fish hooked under that bush.

Thither one fine day came a keen clergyman from Chudleigh. The usual fish was rising under the bush. The parson tried and tried again to get the fly in the right place, and at last made one supreme effort, with the inevitable result that he got hung up in the bush as many a good man had done before. He laid his rod down on the shingle, pulled out his pipe, filled it and lit it, then he strolled leisurely down to the footbridge, which he crossed, then up Preston main street until he came to the first cottage gate; here he went in, and through the garden to a path that wound its way to the lower garden by the river. He unhooked his fly from the bush and threw it into the river to float across, when the unexpected happened.

Up came the fish with a proper head and tail rise, took the fly and made off downstream. The parson was for a moment dumbfounded, then the scream of the reel woke him into action. Up the zig-zag path he went at record pace, down the street, across the footbridge he pounded, then a hundred yards' sprint to where the rod was.

Oh, how he wished he was forty years younger. Just as he reached the rod there was a violent jerk, and the backing of the line broke off where he had tied it to the reel. Away went the fish, fly cast, and one hundred and ten yards of line and backing, never to be seen again. But if he had only kept his head and waded across the river just below the bridge the odds are he would have hit on the line, but this did not suggest itself to him.

Late one afternoon J. and I were in a third class carriage in a train returning from fishing, when, as we pulled up at Chudleigh Station, we saw the same reverend gentleman standing on the platform with his rod up. We beckoned to him and he came over to us and began to talk about the state of the river.

Just as the guard blew his whistle the large minnow, which he had on, and which was hitched in the lower ring of his rod, came loose and swung into the window of our carriage, fastening itself firmly into the cushion. Before we could disengage it, the train started. Round went his reel, faster and faster as the train gathered speed. He ran up the platform shouting for all he was worth, and it was not until the train had well cleared the station that the railway officials were able to stop it. We then cut the minnow out but that reverend gentleman, so prone to disaster, would not be my first choice of fishing companion.

Langford Brown, *By the Water's Side*, 1936

Acrobatic Fish

WHEN fresh fish are running, what vagaries they have. I have seen them throw themselves so far out of the water as to fall on dry ledges of rocks; and when you hook a fresh-run fish, what fearful leaps he will take.

I had a curious adventure that exemplifies this. I hooked a fresh-run salmon in a deep pool seldom fished, because it was supposed to be unprolific of sport; he made a rush right across the pool and threw a most tremendous somersault, landing himself upon a ledge of rock at least two feet higher than the water on the opposite bank, and there he lay for a few seconds without moving, no doubt as much astonished at his position as I was.

However, he soon found that dry land was not his place and he jumped himself back again, and as quick as lightning rushed across the pool to where I was standing, one foot on one rock and one on another, with a small and fast and deep stream of water running between the rocks. Before I could wind him up, he went right between my legs and down through the gully. How I turned I know not, but he was away over rocks and shallows, with his back out of the water, to a pool about one hundred yards below.

Unfortunately, he was not well hooked and although the line cleared all obstacles, I had no time to wind up short or get a strain on him. No sooner had I reached his new pool below than he set off for the next, to which I could not follow. And thus did I lose the most acrobatic fish a man ever hooked!

Edward Hamilton, Fly Fishing, 1884

Double Trouble

I HOOKED a salmon on the Bandon at Cork, but I'd been fishing for trout and had on the lightest tackle imaginable. Three flies on the thinnest gut. As soon as the salmon took me I knew I was in trouble but, after his first rush, I thought I had a chance.

He shook his head, made a second run and leaped clear of the water.

Ten pounds I thought. The fight continued. I saw his silver flank in mid-stream. He was tiring, but then, unbelievably, I saw the ghostly shadow of another salmon just behind the hooked fish. Almost at once I realised what was about to happen – and happen it did. The second fish took one of my other flies and set off in the opposite direction to the first fish.

Miraculously, for a few seconds I was aware of both fish still on the line, then, inevitably, they were gone. No one I spoke to in the long years after that incident could ever recall a similar occurrence.

Richard Greene, It's Later Than You Think, 1888

Eels and Ears

BEING LATE for the mayfly was rather a failing of mine, for on another occasion, being invited to fish a well-known stretch of the Test, I arrived again the day after the fairest fishing.

A fellow guest and I were detailed to the upper water, and to beguile the time I fished for dace, to my companion's barely concealed scorn. However, as the dace rose and took well, he asked if he could have a similar fly to mine, so I made a cast on to his bank, and he removed the fly, and by lunchtime we had a marvellous basket of large dace. There was another guest, who had never fished before, and to this day I am still wondering whether he really believed that they were Test trout.

It was here that one day I saw an eel come out from beneath a piece of corrugated iron in one of the hatchery pools and seize a small trout; after lunch we netted the eel with half of the trout still projecting from its jaws. The trout, already partially digested, was four inches long and the eel about a pound.

On another occasion on the Kennet, while throwing a long line with a strong following breeze, I felt a hard blow upon one of my ears, then noticed that my mayfly was gone, and quite a casual examination located it in my ear, with the barb well through. As it was cold there was no pain, so another fly was attached, but no rise was to be seen, so the rod was leant against a fence and I sat down to wait. Suddenly the rapid revolutions of my reel caused me to jump up, and hastily collecting the rod and climbing the fence, I set off at my best pace to try and retrieve my fly, at the moment stuck fast in the rump of a cow. The cow kept the fly.

I solicited the aid of the landlady on my return to lunch to try to remove the barb of the fly in my ear, and a poor job she made of it; pulling me around the room as she tried to extract the hook by brute force while I howled with pain. Eventually she gave me the wire cutters and the hook was cut and out.

Richard Lake, *Fishing Memories*, 1928

Flying Sea Trout

I REACHED the river and discovered the colonel playing a fish. He said he was fed up with it, as he had had it on for a long time, and would be very glad if I could help. I had a short net with me and, finding out where the fish was, I climbed out on the alder bushes over the river, which looked deep just there. I held on with my left hand and got the fish in the net with my right hand, but then I was done. I did not want to get a ducking, and, of course, I could not use my right hand as I had the net in it with the sea trout; neither could I move my left hand, with which I was hanging on. I asked the Colonel if he would risk the fish, and he said, 'Yes, I must, as the bush will not bear both of us.' I then said, 'All right, slack off everything – I am going to try to throw the net and fish back over my head and the bushes.' I managed to do it, but as the net sailed through the air the sea trout – all six pounds of it – dropped cleanly into the water.

Edward Hamilton, *Fly Fishing*, 1884

Torn to Shreds

I ONCE had a most distressing experience with a salmon on the Teign. H. and I were walking up the river and had got about ten yards below the footbridge that leads to Preston village when we saw a fish rise under the other bank. It was late on in the year, the end of September, and nothing had been done lately, therefore to see a fish move was quite an event.

I tried to persuade H. to go over the bridge and try for this fish, which could not be got at from the side we were on as he was lying right under the bank on the other side, below a huge dead stump that hung over the river, and the stream would not let a fly pass over him.

H. refused point blank to go over to try the fish; whether he foresaw future trouble I do not know, but I expect he did. So I went over myself, and to my horror I found that there was a large patch of brambles about eighty yards long by five or six yards wide, with the big stump halfway down.

With much trouble and considerable trepidation, I climbed out on the stump, which felt very unsafe, as it rocked about with my weight.

After a few casts I hooked the fish, and H. who was watching from the other bank, said he would come round. By the time he arrived the fish was getting done, and he began to look for a place where he could land it. He spotted a place some forty yards below as the only possible one. I therefore had to force my way through that awful tangle of brambles that was as high as my waist.

Oh, what a state my legs and hands were in. I was torn to shreds and bleeding badly. It was very many days before I was again comfortable and able to fish. True I got the fish – all six pounds of him – but I do not think he was worth the cuts and lacerations I suffered as he had been a very long time in the river and was a very long way from being a fresh fish.

Richard Lake, Fishing Memories, 1928

Salmon Tied in Knots

JUST ABOVE Head Weir on the Mole is a very deep, still pool some hundred yards in length. In it are collected a great many snags of all sizes that have been brought down by the river when in spate.

One stormy, blustering afternoon I was fishing this place with an eleven-foot trout rod with two flies on the cast, in the hope of getting hold of a sea trout. It was very awkward fishing, as there was an alder hedge some three feet six inches between me and the river. Just as I made a cast, there came a gust of wind that blew my very light line right under the hedge on my side of the river. As the tail fly landed on the water something took it and made off into the middle of the pool.

My wife was sketching about a hundred yards away and, on my shouting to her, she came running down. 'What have you got hold of there?' she said. I replied that I did not know, but it was something big. I also told her that she need not get excited, as our chance of landing whatever it was about nil in this pool, with all its snags.

After a little we saw that it was a fish that had taken the fly. I had, of course, to let him go just where he liked, as I was using very fine tackle. However, all went well for about a quarter of an hour, when he made a run downstream of some forty yards. In doing this he passed under the root of an oak stump that was lying on the bottom of the river some five or six feet out from my bank. I got my wife to pull me a stick out of the hedge that had a fork to it. I then gave her the rod, and, holding the line in my left hand, I went cautiously into the water up to my neck. Fortunately, the fish was lying quite still below. After poking about for several minutes with the stick I managed to free the line: I then came out of the water, took the rod and walked downstream, reeling in as I went. When I got some forty yards down I could see the fish quite plainly, as the water was very clear: he was quite still, standing on his head with his tail up. I watched him for a minute or so, and as he did not move I again went into the water with a big net I had with me and quietly lifted him out.

Great was our astonishment – and my disappointment – when we got him on the bank, only to discover that he was stone dead. On examination, we found that he was properly hooked with the tail fly, but the cast was wound six times around his head, thus tying up his mouth and also his gills, the dropper fly being firmly hooked in the fish's side, about a foot above the tail.

My wife is most positive that when the fish went through the loop of the oak stump this fly was free, as she saw it. The only way to account for the fish having wound himself up in this manner, to my mind, is that when he was left alone while I was freeing the line he must have been rolling about and so wound himself up. I still have the cast with the two flies and a photograph of the fish, which was fourteen pounds.

One does not always get off so easily if a fish goes through a loop. I was one day fishing a little higher up the river and I hooked a small fish of seven or eight pounds. A man who was breaking stones by the road came to help me, but he badly missed the fish with the tailer and before he could get another shot the fish got through a loop, caused by a root growing out from the bank, and in again. This fish broke me.

Near the same spot, one night when fishing for sea trout when it was practically dark, I had a very curious experience. I hooked something under water that went off at once downstream for about sixty yards at a most terrific speed and broke me, because apparently the reel could not revolve fast enough. I feel certain that it was no fish, as no fish could have gone at that speed. I have always thought that it was an otter or something bigger and more mysterious that I would not hazard to guess at. But one thing is certain – its speed was extraordinary and it snapped my line like cotton thread. My reel span so fast it burned my thumb and my rod had a permanent kink in it ever after that disastrous encounter.

Richard Lake, *Fishing Memories,* 1928

The Weed Not the Man

FATHER B. was the Roman Catholic priest at Fort George. He was an extremely popular man and often he used to dine at the Mess. I used to love to hear him tell the story as to how he was fishing for salmon with a minnow in Loch Ness. He said that he hooked a fish that immediately dived into very deep water, from which he could not shift him although he tried all he knew.

Being a very patient man and very keen to catch the fish, he sat in the boat for two hours, and at last the fish came up entangled in a lot of weed, quite dead. I suppose it had been choked by the weed. The weight of the fish was thirty pounds, and the old man's eyes used to fairly sparkle as he told the tale but it was a sad tale too because he always felt the weed had caught the fish not the man.

Richard Lake, Fishing Memories, 1928

An Endless Dive, and Then Rain

IT WAS a beautiful August evening on Loch Monar, warm and still, and the loch was like a sheet of glass. I remember that the high mountains that surrounded the loch were all reflected in it upside down. I have never seen the like of this before and I have never seen it since.

There was a large hatch of fly, and the trout were rising readily. I went off by myself in a boat and started to fish for these trout with a dry fly. I shortly caught three or four about three-quarters of a pound apiece and then I hooked one very much larger. This fellow at once dived down, taking out a lot of line, right under the boat.

I had him on for several minutes, and then, as I could not manage the boat properly and play the fish at the same time, I was badly broken, losing the whole of my cast so I could no longer fish at all.

I have often wondered how deep this trout really went, but his dive at the time seemed endless and terrifying and no power of mine could move him.

I have never fished Loch Monar except for this short period of about an hour and a half and it ended in general chaos, for that night it started to rain and it rained for a whole week without stopping, and the loch, large as it is, rose so that all the boats that were moored in the boathouse were sunk. No fishing was possible at all. Perhaps the reflection of the mountains that I saw had been a sort of warning of this coming storm.

J. H.Vahey, *The Humane Angler,* 1910

Inglorious Piking

TO BEGIN. Down at the pool by twelve – not a trout would run: twisted my ribs with throwing, till they were nearly off, and over and over again in the flushes and shallows and mill. Went to that side by the willows – got a run – found a heavy fish –gut and gear soon bit off.

A little after, evidently got hold of the same animal again; played him with the lightest hand some time, and at last softly came the hooks away, without bait being apparently touched, and nothing whatever damaged.

Went away to rest, and then back for the jack pike: got hold of a fellow as heavy as a trunk of a tree (evidently that same old friend who destroys us every time); could never bring him near the top, and after certain gentle fighting he went to the deepest part of the water, and there remained fixed.

No twitching would move him, and pulling would have been destruction. At length Shepherd proposed and got the punt, and in it we went; but I must tell you, before we got to his stronghold he exhibited his proportions by a jump a yard and a half of length. When in the punt, we could move him off by the pole, and away he went towards the shallows and willow side of the pool. When there, I lightly tried to bring him towards the boat and net; but in an instant, when he found himself thus circumstanced, he rushed off again to the deep, and there lay like a log. Of course (and very ticklish work it was) we displaced him again, and occasionally, when opportunity offered, turned him by heading him from his place of refuge; this could very seldom be done, and thus for more than one hour and a half we fought him.

At last, when he was lying loggish fifteen feet down, Shepherd was obliged to put the longest pole close to him. Off he rushed, and, oh sad, when about a rod and a half's length away, up came the gut, soft and short.

I was not conscious of giving him the smallest check by my left hand, through which the line passed;

and I kept line ready; and consequently suppose either he bit or rubbed off the gut, or got it round some piece of wood at the bottom. The incessant working in the line I mention was no joke to either Shepherd or myself. I judge him from twenty to thirty pounds. What a triumph had I caught him but I know not, with single gut, how it could be done, for he would not keep moving so as to be tired and tractable.

Sir Herbert Maxwell

(Ed) *Chronicles of the Houghton Fishing Club, 1822–1908,* 1908

Chapter 5

HEAD OVER HEELS

The Great Unseen Bass

IT IS four o'clock on a July morning. The sun is still down behind Exmouth but as we walk a few steps to the boathouse the haze that broods over the den, the cloudless blue sky overhead, the stillness in the air, all forecast a scorching day. A little after four, having aroused Cox, who like the May Queen has to be wakened early if he is to get up at all, and given him time for his inevitable cup of stewed syrupy tea, we are snug in the Hirondelle, our trout rods and traces of single gut ready for action. It will be high water soon after nine.

We shoot out from the landing place and just above us lie great merchantmen in tiers, flying the flags of half a dozen nations. As we first approach the lowermost tier, however, all is silence. We cannot drift the way we like until the tide runs swifter, so Cox will for forty minutes or so row the boat slowly and in circles abreast of these lower ships and the railway quay. We shall not hook anything large, but our baits are over the side now, and one never knows.

Ha! What was that? A twitch of the rod top ... another ... down it goes, for the slight turn of the wrist has nicked the sharp hook in beyond the barb, and the bass is fast. The reel sings a modulated hymn of praise, not raising its voice as it would if turned by a heavier fish; and the slender rod bobs, not indeed with the steady curve that tells of a big one, but sufficiently to suggest a pounder.

To bring such a bass to the net is child's work. In vain it eddies and circles around the stern. The little bronze reel is wound in almost without a hitch, and at just the right moment Cox has shipped his oars and dipped the landing net under a gleaming little bass of perhaps a pound and a half.

One does not fetch out the steelyard to these small fry, although such a fish is as pretty and as sporting as any of its size. Trout, someone murmurs? Speak up; and remember that, though we use a trout rod, the cast is of salmon gut, for to trust to anything finer would be to run needless risk with that record fish of the season, to dream of which means inexpensive bliss.

Hook a bass like him that lies shining in the boat, quieted with the merciful tap of a rowlock, on a moorland trout cast; hook him, if you like, but play him in a bath if you want him, for he would break your gossamer gut for all your arts. Another sand eel on the hook, and once more to turn our back on Cox, who again dips the paddles gently in the stream. Three or four more bass, a little smaller than the first, are hooked during the next half hour. And now the salt water is flooding the estuary in earnest; the boat drifts yards upstream each time Cox drops the sculls for the landing net; and away now to the rough ground, just below the bridge, where, undisturbed by the salmon nets, the big bass lie in wait for the shoals of brit that come, reckless of their doom, on the rising tide.

As we pass the topmost ships, with only a couple of yachts between us and the bridge, the dripping bait box is hauled inside the boat, and the largest sand eels are picked out from the wriggling mass, for big bass like big fare, and if the giants are to be tempted, we must offer them the best we have.

Instead of trailing the bait, as I did for the smaller game below, I now pay it out, little by little, an inch or two of the line being pulled off the reel at a time. This I go on doing mechanically, while Cox just dips the paddles so as to keep the boat back ever so little, that the line may run out as straight as a wire. Past the tennis courts we go, looking through the arches of the bridge at the purple line of the tors on Dartmoor, and now the baits must be thirty yards away from us.

There is a slight check, the merest irregularity, which would not be noticed by anyone new to the game, but which we know so well that instinctively the left hand tightens on the butt, while the right hovers above the reel. There it is! Down goes the top, no bobbing this time, but the deliberate curve to the water's edge.

'Murder!' screams the winch, no half-hearted burr of the check like that evoked by the little fish, but a sustained crescendo note, while the line grows so rapidly less on the spinning axle that it looks as if the fish is going to break me.

Once, and once only, thank goodness, that did actually befall me on this spot. What manner of fish it may have been, I cannot, without having a glimpse of it, positively say. Local opinion favoured a salmon, but more probably it was a monster 'cobbler' bass. It simply took the bait by the lowest buoys, opposite the cricket ground, started away at lightning speed, and, as the song says, 'never stopped running till it got home'. It ran two yards of gut and one hundred yards of line to their full limit without a pause and then, without apparent effort, went on, fortunately breaking the line so near the hook that my loss of tackle was small. Other bass I have lost in that stream, but that is the first and last so massive that it fought invisible.

The fish that I have hooked here by the buoy, although a powerful fighter, is not an adversary of such extreme mettle, for already he has halted in his mad career, a respite of which I take advantage to reel in half a dozen yards. Steady there! A fish of such size must be wound in gingerly, with caution, and the hand must be ever on and off the winch, winding only when the fish is so minded, since at this early stage of the struggle a direct clash of wills would mean disaster.

Away goes the bass again, with strength renewed by its brief rest. Its yielding was but a feint, and this time it runs out twice as much line as I reeled in, and so is further from the boat than ever. Another halt, another reeling in, and now we are nearly up to the bridge, for all the time the boat has drifted along.

For a moment I am undecided whether to shoot through the middle arch and land the fish above the bridge, but that means losing time, so, 'This side,' Cox I say; and Cox understands, with the knowledge born of many such encounters, that he is to back the boat into the shallows on the railway side.

It is there, under the windows of the early train, that the last stand is made. Gallantly the bass disputes every yard, for he is fighting for his last chance now, and he knows it. Gradually, and with fewer interruptions, I get the fine line back on the reel, and now his green head can be seen on the surface, shaking the worrying hook, as a terrier shakes a rat, and now and then making a futile attempt at retreat. In vain, such tactics. The line is tested, the hook tempered; and at last, with a final protest that spins the reel for twenty revolutions, the fish rolls on his side, and the ready landing net is beneath it, the handle straining with the weight as Cox lifts what looks like a good ten-pounder over the side. A powerful fish, even out of the water; and the head has to be gripped firmly between the knees while the hook is taken out of the angle of the jaw, and the steelyard, confirmed later when we got ashore, registers eleven and a quarter pounds, a noble fish and the best I ever took on the rod in that river.

But perhaps always such fish are a ghostly reminder of the great ones we have lost – and immediately comes to mind that unseen bass lost years earlier; a bass so powerful that no rod and line it seems could ever hold him.

F. G. Aflalo, *The Salt of my Life,* 1905

'I am Afraid it is a Shark'

WE TRAVELLED to Marco, a little settlement fringed round with coconut palms, one stormy afternoon in a small boat, and we spent that night at a little store, a rough shanty, but well equipped nevertheless. One could purchase all the needs of a rude civilisation at this place. The Seminole Indians obtain many of their goods there, and give in exchange skins of their own tanning, some most admirably prepared.

Our company was rough and much of the type so well described by Bret Harte and other Western authors.

Still, our host did his best to make us comfortable, and his little daughter rose early to prepare us a breakfast. Afterwards we proceeded with our guide, Tom Hart, a man who can always be heard of at Marco, who knows the whole coast well and is an admirable fellow, to a spot at which, the previous year, he assisted to land three fish in a single day.

Our lunch consisted of green coconuts, a small sackful of Florida oranges, cold venison (venison is the staple diet in this part of Florida), biscuits, together with many bottles of ginger ale that we had brought with us; for this part of Florida is under the Prohibition Law.

The morning opened grandly. It was perfectly calm, the sunshine was brilliant, and I was strongly reminded of the Nile on a March day. Yet Hart was dissatisfied. As we made our way up the beautiful creek, I looked at as much of the horizon as I could see, but there was not so much as a cloud of the size of a man's hand. We proceeded in a leisurely manner, stopping now and then to dip our great palmetto hats into the water, in order that we might keep our heads a little cool, for the heat even at ten o'clock was almost too much for endurance.

We had gone about a mile, and Hart was resting on his oars for a moment, when on a sudden, within three feet of the boat, there was a huge swish and swirl – a miniature maelstrom for a moment – and there appeared a great black back and huge projecting fin.

'Tarpon,' said Hart.

It was my first sight of a big fish, and I must

frankly confess that I felt nervous when I looked at my comparatively small rod and its frail line. He must have been a daring fellow who first thought of hooking a tarpon with rod and reel. Presently, the excitement of the sport was upon me. We went as rapidly as possible up the creek and anchored under the lee of an island. During the night Hart had gone out with his casting net and captured a couple of dozen mullet, varying in size from twelve to eighteen inches. In an instant he had his knife out, and we baited up with mullet heads, a favourite of the bigger tarpon.

Hart threaded the hook through the bait with a large skewer, attached the leather trace to the line, and cast for me – not a long cast, perhaps twenty-five or thirty yards. The bait sank to the bottom, and I sat with the check off the reel, and some loose line gathered in the boat, awaiting events.

It was early yet. Now and then in the distance you could see a great swirl in the water, and a tarpon rose, but they kept clear of our boat. We sat smoking in the brilliant sunshine, and at the end of twenty minutes I reeled in and found that my bait had been swallowed by a huge shellfish, a conch. It weighed between seven and eight pounds, and we had to cut it open before we could get the hook out of it. It was not unlike a gigantic whelk. This was an amusing but not a brilliant beginning.

We put on fresh bait, moved forty or fifty yards, and cast in again. The day was getting hotter, and the big fish began to rise (for air) very numerously. After a time, we took to counting the rises, and I am not exaggerating when I say that within sight of my field-glasses – we could see close upon a mile in one direction – more than fifty distinct black fins showed during that morning. Another cigar, another mullet head bait, a fresh cast, and we settled down to watch the dial of my reel.

I found Hart a pleasant and remarkably well informed person. There were few modern books of adventure with which he was not acquainted, although not many authors could have produced a more exciting tale than the history of this man's life, spent as it was in exploring the vast unknown recesses of the Everglades in search of the egret's plumes, with which fashionable ladies adorn their hats and hair.

His existence had been hard and solitary, and, although he is now attaining a certain prosperity, he has spent some thousands of nights camping out alone in that strange snake- and panther-ridden country. Our chat is cut short, however, by a sudden disappearance of the loose line over the side of the boat. Then the reel began to run out like lightning. The excitement of the moment was terrific. One's first salmon, one's first tarpon, one's first trout, are, I should imagine, the most tremendous moments in a career of sport.

I struck, and within some fifty yards from the boat but in quite a contrary direction from that in which the line was running out, a monster fish leapt from the water. Immediately at the beginning of the run Hart had pulled up the anchor and we were drifting. When he saw the direction in which the fish had leapt he looked grave. The line, covered with seaweed, had sagged tremendously: he feared that the fish had dropped the bait, and he was right.

I wound up and found that my intended victim had seized the mullet and, in that curious way fish have, had ejected it some feet up the line. We were gloomy and disappointed.

Still, the day was young and the fish were rising numerously, although it is by some guides not considered a good sign when they are on the top of the water. I cast in again, and almost before the bait had got to the bottom it was taken. When the correct one hundred yards of the reel line had run out, I struck. There was a vast commotion at the top of the water, although not exactly a leap, and we were convinced I was in for a tarpon, and a massive one at that.

The fish, whatever it was, swam hither and thither at lightning speed, and then on a sudden it stopped. I struck again, knowing that if it were a tarpon it would then like as not rise to the top and leap. It did not do so.

'I am afraid it is a shark, sir,' remarked my guide. My heart sank.

I can assure those who have never hooked a shark on a line that this particular fish gave me any amount of trouble. Hart rowed as fast as he could, and I reeled in rapidly to gain line, for woe betide the tarpon or shark fisher if his line is overrun. I got within probably thirty yards of the fish, when he was off again, and he ran down a branch creek for close upon half a mile. A big shark can tow a boat a very considerable distance; but there seems to be one way of tiring him, and that is, to get to one side of him, and then, using one's rod as a lever, swing round and pull against him with all one's force. In course of time that seems to exhaust him, and, revolver ready, one can reel him in, cut the line and let him go or shoot him through the nose.

My shark was evidently tired when we got up to him, and I could see his great seven-foot body looming green and hideous beneath the water. What a terrifying looking monster a shark is!

As I drew him up I thought he was practically dead. But he suddenly lashed the water furiously, and the reel, upon which I had put the check, gave such a screech as I have never heard from any reel before. He ran out some hundred and fifty yards of line, but as I drew up to him again he was obviously getting tired. There is a mental process in angling that enables one to know when one has at last gained mastery of one's fish, and so it was with this shark. I got him up to the top of the water again. He made a violent struggle when he saw the boat, but this time we were able to cut the line and he was gone.

By this time, we had wandered completely out of our course. No tarpon were known to be in the water near us, and we were thinking of returning; but despite the bright sunshine a change had come over the weather, and I know of no part of the world in which the weather alters more rapidly than in southern Florida. The wind was sighing in the mangrove trees, and although the sun shone as brightly as ever, the air grew strangely chilly. By the time we had gone back the mile we had lost, Hart was despondent. There were no tarpon rising. All we could see was a great porpoise, which rose within a few yards of us, blowing as emphatically as a steam engine.

'I am afraid we shall get no more sport today,' remarked Hart. And he was right. We fished for another hour until the storm had come upon us, and then we turned back to Marco. My dream of a giant tarpon was over.

A. C. Harmsworth,
quoted in John Bickerdyke's *Sea Fishing,* 1895

Shark Bait Tarpon
Lokoja, West Africa, 1914

DEAR CHARLES, you will see from my address that I am travelling again. As a matter of fact, I am on my way back from Lagos where I have been for a couple of months on special work. I had quite a good time, plenty to do in the day-time and free week-ends to do what I liked in.

Lagos is the same as ever, hasn't changed one little bit from the first time I went there, four years ago.

Naturally, I hadn't been there long before I began poking about to see if anybody had been sea fishing, but still found the same blissful ignorance as prevailed on my last visit. Harbour works certainly very much extended, but I hear they are getting trouble with silting and will have to build out an easterly arm – some job, looks for life.

I found the same old native fisherman who catered for me on my first visit, and my general purpose man got busy and found me a dugout that would take me out fishing. This was an opportunity not to be despised, so I clinched the arrangements entered into by Hassan, my man.

One trouble was that I know very little of their language, and they couldn't understand a word of Hausa, the language I know fairly well. However, Hassan seems to be able to make known my wants. I used my heaviest greenheart spinning rod and largest spinning reel with heavy wire traces, and my home-made spinners, the gear I had been using for the big Giwan Rua, so felt really ready for the big stuff.

The first time we went out from the breakwater we began trolling, with the sea beautifully calm and as blue as turquoise under the early morning sun. Both men paddled well with long, easy strokes, quite different from our up river boys, so that my bait did its work properly. I was so eager to begin that I hadn't really had time to get my few things put shipshape when I got such a wrench on the rod. I grabbed it of course and nearly turned the canoe over. These canoes are very gimcrack affairs with only a foot freeboard, no keel, just hewn out of a tree with rough shapings for a bow and a stern. I sit flat in the bottom, facing astern, as I cannot kneel for long periods like my men do. My fish went completely away, going so fast that my rod top was drawn down into the sea, and I could not for the life of me hold him, although I had the palm of my hand on the rim of the revolving drum of the reel until it nearly burnt into the flesh. I was only too glad when the fish stopped and I could get my rod up to a safe angle. Almost before I could get my wits together, the fish came towards me and passed right under the canoe. I seemed to reel for hours before the rod bent violently and away he went again.

This went on for ages, until I began to feel really annoyed that I couldn't subdue him. I put every bit of my strength into it until I thought the rod couldn't have stood the strain any longer, but would have gone at one of the joints. This, I think, really took all the strength out of him, and we got him so near that I could see his dim shape weaving about below us. He turned to and fro, but had to come up and was got on board by Hassan. I was fully convinced that I had hooked the father of all whales, but the fish didn't weigh more than thirty-two pounds when we weighed him. He was a deep fish, slate blue on top, with a blunt head and finlets like a mackerel, also the forked tail of that family. Here I had been nearly an hour over this small fish, and was thoroughly done, so what was I going to be like if I got into a real big one, which was my idea in life at that time? However, this was much better than our previous experiences.

When I was having a rest I saw a lot of silvery looking fish jumping out of the water. They jumped out in a flock, so we went over to have a look. These fish, I should judge, were from six to twelve inches in length, swimming together in shoals. I was watching them with interest, really thinking what excellent bait they would be, when we saw a great rush into the middle of them, and out came the flock, wildly leaping from their pursuers.

This meant business, so I rigged up another bait, and the two men took the dugout around the outskirts of the shoal. I could see down in the clear water dark blue shapes flashing underneath, so let the bait down astern. I distinctly saw three go for my bait; one got it, and away he went, but I only saw the belly flash of the other two out of the corner of my eye, as I had on my hands quite enough trouble for the immediate future. I never dreamt a fish had so much strength. When I tried to hold him he pulled yards off with savage primitive tugs. The upper three-quarters of my rod was horizontal to the water with the strain, and I held on, feeling quite a void round my heart region. When nearly two hundred yards had gone he stopped, but before I could congratulate myself he was away again, but this time my canoe boys had got the hang of things and gave me help by following the fish. At the end of the second run my fish came clear out of the water and tugged until the line twanged and vibrated with the strain. I couldn't help letting out a yell.

The fish never eased up, and I finally fought him back by instinct and not with a reasoning mind. I was really feeling physically distressed when I realised he was near the canoe and Hassan got him out. This was a different fish from the other. He was long and slim like a torpedo, blue black on top with a silver belly flushed with yellow right down to the tail, which was forked like a mackerel, and I am sure this fish is the American Yellowtail. He was forty-five pounds when weighed, and I truly had had enough, especially as we were too far from land for my liking. The men paddled for the shore while I got my strength back. With these two magnificent fish on board I really couldn't bear to put a bait over and have another shot. I was sitting watching the water when, bang, I had another run, and the business began all over again, but this fish fought deep down nearly under the canoe and I felt that this might indeed be the record breaker I had so long sought. I was in a state of high excitement such as I have never experienced before.

The battle was immense and exhausting but at last I was fairly on top of my fish when he suddenly woke up and ran yards off. I gave him hell but could not make any impression, although he was coming up to the surface with a rush. I was watching the rod tip when Hassan, with a chorus from the other men, yelled and pointed to a big fin sticking out of the water about one hundred yards away. I realised that the owner of that fin and myself were connected in some way and also that it was not the huge fish I had assumed but instead a shark. It took about three seconds to overcome my disappointment and for my mind to go over all the shark incidents I had ever read about. I was not comforted. Still, something had to be done, as the shark wasn't doing anything much, and the only place my men wanted to go to was Home, Sweet Home in the shortest time possible. I therefore held hard, and nothing occurred. I might be holding hard until now for all the good I was doing. However, things did move; the line went slack, and the fin moved out seawards. I reeled in with a huge sigh and soon saw I was reeling in not the shark I feared but the head and shoulders only of my massive fish; the other part was going seawards with the shark.

However, our troubles were only beginning, as when the fish's head got near a great shape came from under the canoe. My fish's head and shoulders disappeared into the shape, and my reel began to spin round faster than anybody could have thought possible.

I had really and truly hooked a shark this time, but what the devil to do with him I hadn't the foggiest notion. There may be a book written on shark fishing to help soft-headed amateurs like myself when in such trouble, but if there is I have never read it. I simply clung on for all my life. Then the brute began to run. I felt a tremendous jar on my left arm and shoulders, the dugout gave a lurch, and my rod came back straight.

I never said 'Thank God' with such thankfulness before, and believed every letter of those two small words. I was feeling pretty frightened, but on turning round with a sickly grin I found three absolutely terrified guides; so I took courage as I realised there were three more frightened men in my little world than I myself. There was no more fishing, and no urging was wanted on my part until we arrived at the shore. My legs felt quite shaky on landing, so we found a shady spot and had lunch. Through Hassan I had a long talk with the men and finally, after treating them well in the matter of a monetary present, got them to promise they would be there the next Sunday. They took the yellowtail, whilst I took the other fish, which was quite good eating. I felt the effects next day on my shoulders, and also in my groin, where the butt of the rod rested during my fishing. I therefore tied a piece of stuffed leather as big as a tennis ball on to the butt end of the rod to act as a cushion, and it was a great success, but even then there is a danger that one might hurt one's inside.

When out the next Sunday morning we didn't get any luck at all until we saw a school of small fish being crashed, and, as soon as we could troll a bait around the school, I got a run, which resulted in a twenty-five pound yellowtail. By the time the fight was over the school had either gone a long distance out to sea or gone down for good.

Owing to my crazy craft, I was frightened to go out far to sea in case of accidents, as if we got upset there were too many sharks, so we kept as near to the bar as possible. This day I saw some fish leaping clear out of the water in magnificent jumps, so we trolled around the neighbourhood and got into one without much difficulty. There was a terrific long run, and then out of the water and up into the air came five feet of silver. The fish seemed to my astonished eyes to go up and up, but when he came down again the line was slack. On examining the bait, I found the hook of the tail triangle, although it was of large dimension, pulled out straight. I then removed all three triangles and used one large hook, a number ten nought, and again tried my luck. I got another strike, so gave it back to him; another long run, then out of the water again came the fish with his mouth wide open, rattling his gills.

At the top of the jump I saw my hook flung quite another twenty feet into the air. I yelled like an Indian, when the beggar jumped, quite involuntarily. As there seemed quite a number of these fish about working on the bar, I baited up again and got another strike, with a repetition of the jumping performance, but this time the line whistled when he entered the water again. By encouraging my men we settled down to the fight. Seven times the fish came out of the water, sideways, all ways; but I felt he was weakening himself by these acrobatics and felt confident he was ours. The magnificent fish went finally deep and was really coming in when I felt an irresistible force take and shake it like a terrier does a rat. The line went slack, and we got in a bleeding head and a small part of the shoulders only.

I could have wept with annoyance at this further disaster, but could only swear hard to relieve my feelings.

It seems as if every fish as soon as it is weak or fights down will be taken by those accursed sharks. We never got another run. I am convinced these fish that jump are tarpon, as they are just like those described in Dimmock's book of the tarpon; but I did not know they were on this coast.

The dredger Egerton was working on the bar, so I went alongside, and the officers gave me a whisky and soda. It's not my habit to drink before sundown, but I wanted it quite badly. The Egerton officers had been watching my efforts and were greatly interested, but confirmed the shark question. I went home afterwards, real tired.

The next Sunday there were big long swells coming over the bar, so I dared not risk going out in the dugout. I therefore went and fished off the beach into the surf with very little hope of getting anything. I got, however, two good runs and two good fish of a nice size, about twenty pounds each, in the first hour. These fish were of a fine shape, silvery with darker backs, the most noticeable feature being a dull copper colour diffused all over the back of the fish. I wish I had some book that told me what they were. As things were quite bright I was well on the *qui vive* when I felt my bait picked up, then dropped, then picked up again, and the fish moved off with due deliberation. I let him go for ten or fifteen yards, then struck hard. Nothing occurred, and I waited quite a time for action, then struck again. Things then moved, and my fish went sailing majestically parallel to the coast, about seventy yards out, like a tug, and I was forced to trot along the beach after him.

The whole thing was rather ridiculous if there had been an onlooker to see it, but there was only Hassan. Nearly a mile I trotted down the beach, then we returned the same way for some more exercise, until I began to feel a lack of breath; so I stood my ground, only to get a most violent rush that changed the trotting to a fast run. Even then I wasn't holding line. These proceedings went on, I should think, for an hour until I began to see red spots in my eyes. I gave him everything in a desperate effort. I found he was now coming in to me, so I continued until my back nearly broke. On the second breaker we saw a triangular fin and knew our old enemy the shark was around. The next time we surged on the furrow of the wave I realised we had hooked a shark all the time. I felt a real rage, which gave me strength, and I laid into that fish with demoniacal strength until he came in on the last breaker of the surf. What to do with him I didn't know, as I couldn't hold him against the ebb of the surf, and he was done as we saw him roll over several times. The two fishermen with Hassan, however, followed the wave down, got hold of his tail, and, much to my astonishment, with the incoming surf – beached him. I was scared stiff, but they did it off their own bat. My legs shook so much now it was all over that I hastily sat down, while my shoulders ached until I could have shouted. The fit passed off, so I went to see my catch. It was a shark all right, quite ten feet long, grey on the back with a white belly. I judged it a sand shark, but what species I don't know. He must have weighed more than three hundred pounds and was far and away the biggest fish I had ever caught, bigger in fact than my wildest dreams. But I still cursed him and his fellows for destroying my earlier fish.

My rod had a curve in it like a hoop, but it came right again during the week with a weight tied on it and hung up. That ended the day for me. The fishermen took the shark off, after getting aid, and, I believe, sold it piecemeal. Anyway, I got my own back on one of the shark family, but I have no great wish to do it all over again, especially as the tackle that I had is not to my mind suitable for the job. I went out twice more in the dugout. The first time I lost three of the tarpon with sharks; one brute evidently got the hook into his mouth and steamed out towards the open sea. I luckily had a knife and cut adrift before matters became more serious. I lost more than a hundred yards of my twenty-four thread line, which makes things too expensive, especially out here, so I am reduced to trade line, which is really light cord but if dressed is not too bad. I cannot get so much on my reel, which rather cramps my style.

The second time we started out with a tarpon, which changed into a shark. This brute did nothing whatsoever, so we paddled up with great caution. I have ceased to rush things out here. I saw his long grey bulk with the line running to his head, then underneath him, but with no signs of the tarpon. He simply looked at me until my blood ran cold; never moved an eyelid. We got to within fifteen feet of him; that is, he was that much under us, and he was longer than our canoe, which is eighteen feet. I realised with a start what a damned fool I was and how utterly helpless we were, so cut the line in a real good fright. The last I saw of that shark he was in the same position, looking at me with those eyes of his.

It was really quite a time before the hair at the back of my neck went down to its normal position. We went over to the dredger for the needful, which they kindly provided free of cost. Feeling better, we went off towards home, and while on the way hooked a tarpon. At the final tiring of this fish there were three attendant sharks, but they just didn't get him, although one had a good try alongside us – so near that I thought he would overturn us. However, the two men beat the water with their paddles, really in a blue funk – so was I – and Hassan got the tarpon by the gills and heaved him in. One of the sharks followed us in just behind all the way, so my man did not dally that journey.

On landing, I had a good talk to myself about the whole proceedings, and determined that I was every fool under the Sun and not to do it again. My nerves wouldn't stand much more of it. I don't mind having two feet on the sand, but that cranky canoe out there was not good enough. For two nights I had the first nightmares of my life as far as I can remember, and shark's eyes formed too large a portion of them for sound sleep. I took the tarpon to Lagos, where it was weighed – eighty pounds.

Several fellows came to see it, and one of the doctors told me that the natives catch the same fish at Sierra Leone in nets or hand lines – he had forgotten which. It was not good eating at all, so the boys and their friends polished it off. I am very sorry now I didn't dry the head and keep it for a memento. That really finished my fishing, which, I think you will admit, was about as exciting as ever we dreamt about in our wildest dreams. I got on to the mail steamer, went round to Forcados, then up the Niger on a government mail boat without any untold excitement. I shall be here for a short time and then return to my old station, Ibi.

This letter has gone to a most extraordinary length, but I hope you will be interested. I received your letter on spinning for pike, and it did bring back many memories. I shall be returning on leave in November, so it won't be long now before I am fishing the old places with you and Henry.

Hugh Copley, *The Letters of Two Fishermen,* 1930

Chapter 6

MISSING THE POINT

Bovine Battle

IT MUST be clearly understood that I am not at all proud of this performance. In Florida men sometimes hook and land, on rod and tackle a little finer than a steam crane and chain, a mackerel-like fish called 'tarpon' that sometimes run to 120 pounds. Those men stuff their captures, exhibit them in glass cases and become puffed up. On the Columbia River, sturgeon of 150 pounds are taken with the line. When the sturgeon is hooked, the line is fixed to the nearest pine tree or steamboat wharf, and after some hours or days the sturgeon surrenders himself if the pine or line do not give way. The owner of the line then states on oath that he has caught a sturgeon and he too becomes proud. These things are mentioned to show how light a creel will fill the ordinary man with vanity. I am not proud.

It is nothing to me that I have hooked and played several hundred pounds weight of quarry. All my desire is to place the little affair on record before the mists of memory breed the miasma of exaggeration. The minnow cost eighteen pence. It was a beautiful quill minnow, and the tackle-maker said that it could be thrown as a fly. He guaranteed further in respect to the triangles – it glittered with triangles – that, if necessary, the minnow would hold a horse. A man who speaks too much truth is just as offensive as a man who speaks too little. None the less, owing to the defective condition of the present law of libel, the tackle-maker's name must be withheld.

The minnow and I and a rod went down to a brook to attend to a small jack, who lived between two clumps of flags in the most cramped swim that he could select. As a proof that my intentions were strictly honourable, I may mention that I was using a light split cane rod – very dangerous if the line runs through weeds, but very satisfactory in clean water, inasmuch as it keeps a steady strain on the fish and prevents him from taking liberties.

I had an old score against the jack. He owed me two live bait already, and I had reason to suspect him of coming upstream and interfering with a little bleak pool under a horse bridge that lay entirely beyond his sphere of legitimate influence. Observe, therefore, that my tackle and my motives pointed clearly to jack, and jack alone; although I knew that there were monstrous big perch in the brook.

The minnow was thrown as a fly several times, and, owing to my peculiar, and hitherto unpublished, methods of fly throwing, nearly six pennyworth of the triangles came off, either in my coat collar, or my thumb, or the back of my hand.

Fly-fishing is a very gory amusement. The jack was not interested in the minnow, but towards twilight a boy opened a gate of the field and let in some twenty or thirty cows and half-a-dozen carthorses, and they were all very much interested. The horses galloped up and down the field and shook the banks, but the cows walked solidly and breathed heavily, as people breathe who appreciate the fine arts.

By this time I had given up all hope of catching my jack fairly, but I wanted the live bait and bleak account settled before I went away, even if I tore up the bottom of the brook.

Just before I had quite made up my mind to borrow a tin of chloride of lime from the farmhouse – another triangle had fixed itself in my fingers – I made a cast that for pure skill, exact judgement of distance, and perfect coincidence of hand and eye and brain, would have taken every prize at a bait-casting tournament. That was the first half of the cast. The second was postponed because the quill minnow would not return to its proper place, which was under the lobe of my left ear. It had done thus before, and I supposed it was in collision with a grass tuft, till I turned round and saw a large red and white bald-faced cow trying to rub what would be withers in a horse with her nose. She looked at me reproachfully, and her look said as plainly as words: 'The season is too far advanced for gadflies. What is this strange disease?'

I replied, 'Madam, I must apologize for an unwarrantable liberty on the part of my minnow, but if you will have the goodness to keep still until I can reel in, we will adjust this little difficulty.' I reeled in very swiftly and cautiously, but she would not wait. She put her tail in the air and ran away. It was a purely involuntary motion on my part: I struck.

Other anglers may contradict me, but I firmly believe that if a man had foul-hooked his best friend through the nose, and that friend ran, the man would strike by instinct. I struck, therefore, and the reel began to sing just as merrily as though I had caught my jack. But had it been a jack, the minnow would have come away. I told the tackle-maker this much afterwards, and he laughed and made allusions to the guarantee about holding a horse.

Because it was a fat innocent she-cow that had done me no harm the minnow held – held like an anchor fluke in coral moorings – and I was forced to dance up and down an interminable field very largely used by cattle. It was like salmon fishing in a nightmare. I took gigantic strides, and every stride found me up to my knees in

marsh. But the cow seemed to skate along the squashy
green by the brook, to skim over the miry backwaters
and to float like a mist through the patches of rush that
squirted black filth over my face. Sometimes we whirled
through a mob of her friends – there were no friends to
help me – and they looked scandalized; and sometimes
a young and frivolous carthorse would join in the chase
for a few miles, and kick pieces of mud into my eyes;
and through all the mud, the milky smell of kine, the
rush and the smother, I – as aware of my own voice
crying: 'Pussy, pussy, pussy, pretty pussy, come along
then, puss-cat!'

You see it is so hard to speak to a cow properly, and
she would not listen – no, she would not listen. Then she
stopped, and the moon got up behind the pollards to tell
the cows to lie down; but they were all on their feet, and
they came trooping to see.
And she said, 'I haven't had my supper, and I want to go
to bed, and please don't worry me.'

And I said, 'The matter has passed beyond any
apology. There are three courses open to you, my dear
lady. If you'll have the common sense to walk up to my
creel I'll get my knife and you shall have all the minnow.
Or, again, if you'll let me move across to your nearside,
instead of keeping me so coldly on your offside, the
thing will come away in one tweak. I can't pull it out over
your withers. Better still, go to a post and rub it out, dear.
It won't hurt much, but if you think I'm going to lose my
rod to please you, you are mistaken.'

And she said, 'I don't understand what you are saying. I am very, very unhappy.' And I said, 'It's all your fault for trying to fish. Do go to the nearest gatepost, you nice fat thing, and rub it out.'

For a moment I fancied she was taking my advice. She ran away and I followed. But all the other cows came with us in a bunch, and I thought of Phaeton trying to drive the Chariot of the Sun, and Texan cowboys killed by stampeding cattle, and Green Grow the Rushes, Oh and Solomon and Job, and loosing the bands of Orion, and hooking Behemoth, and Wordsworth who talks about whirling round with stones and rocks and trees, and 'Here we go round the Mulberry Bush', and Pippin Hill, and Hey Diddle Diddle, and most especially the top joint of my rod. Again she stopped – but nowhere in the neighbourhood of my knife – and her sisters stood moonfaced round her. It seemed that she might, now, run towards me, and I looked for a tree, because cows are very different from salmon, who only jump against the line, and never molest the fisherman.

What followed was worse than any direct attack. She began to buckjump, to stand on her head and her tail alternately, to leap into the sky, all four feet together, and to dance on her hind legs. It was so violent and improper, so desperately unladylike, that I was inclined to blush, as one would blush at the sight of a prominent statesman sliding down a fire escape, or a duchess chasing her cook with a skillet.

That flopsome abandon might go on all night in the lonely meadow among the mists, and if it went on all night – this was pure inspiration – I might be able to worry through the fishing line with my teeth.

Those who desire an entirely new sensation should chew with all their teeth, and against time, through a best waterproofed silk line, one end of which belongs to a mad cow dancing fairy rings in the moonlight; at the same time keeping one eye on the cow and the other on the top joint of a split cane rod. She buck jumped and I bit on the slack just in front of the reel; and I am in a position to state that that line was cored with steel wire throughout the particular section which I attacked. This has been formally denied by the tackle maker, who is not to be believed. The wheep of the broken line running through the rings told me that henceforth the cow and I might be strangers. I had already bidden goodbye to some tooth or teeth; but no price is too great for freedom of the soul.

'Madam,' I said, 'the minnow and twenty feet of very superior line are your alimony without reservation. For the wrong I have unwittingly done to you I express my sincere regret. At the same time, may I hope that Nature, the kindest of nurses, will in due season, make amends.'

She, or one of her companions, must have stepped on her spare end of the line in the dark, for she bellowed wildly and ran away, followed by all the cows. I hoped the minnow was disengaged at last; and before I went away looked at my watch, fearing to find it nearly midnight.

My last cast for the jack was made at 6.23pm. There lacked still three and a-half minutes of the half-hour, and I would have sworn that the moon was paling before the dawn.

'Simminly someone were chasing they cows down to bottom o 'Ten Acre', said the farmer that evening. 'Twasn't you, sir?'

'Now under what earthly circumstances do you suppose I should chase your cows? I wasn't fishing for them, was I?'

Then all the farmer's family gave themselves up to laughter for the rest of the evening, because that was a rare and precious jest, and it was repeated for months, and the fame of it spread from that farm to another, and yet another at least three miles away, and it will be used again for the benefit of visitors when the freshets come down in spring.

But to the greater establishment of my honour and glory I submit in print this bald statement of fact, that I may not, through forgetfulness, be tempted later to tell how I hooked a bull on a Marlow Buzz, how he ran up a tree and took to water, and how I played him along the London road for thirty miles, and netted him at Smithfields. Errors of this kind may creep in with the lapse of years, and it is my ambition ever to be a worthy member of that fraternity who pride themselves on never deviating by one hair's breadth from the absolute and literal truth.

Rudyard Kipling, *Short Stories*, 1910

Just One Thing
After Another ...

IT IS mercifully ordained that one's keenest memories are in general of things pleasant. The angler in reminiscent mood loves to dwell on big baskets, soft western breezes, and the other outstanding features of a roseate past.

The things he has suffered in the pursuit of his recreation have left but little impression behind, and in retrospect seem but little clouds on the mental horizon. This is as it should be, for if the remembrance of pains and disasters were as vivid as the remembrance of pleasures, a man would seriously begin to wonder whether it was all worthwhile.

Yet, in spite of this beneficent ordinance of fate, there must be always days in one's angling history that one still regards with horror and indignation – days that no amount of subsequent joy has availed to obliterate.

It has always seemed to me that an undue number of them falls to my share, but this may not be a real philosophical discovery, for I have heard other men complain, apparently with some reason. The worst days of all I group roughly together; they represent the limited number of occasions on which I have sworn a solemn oath to give up fishing for ever. In addition to their own inherent vileness they must, therefore, also bear the responsibility of several solemn oaths having been broken, although this last is not a charge that I would wish to press too seriously. It would have been a pity if an oath made in haste of an evening had seemed more than an expression of impatience at breakfast time on the morrow. Only once do I remember really giving up fishing in consequence of a malign day, and in agreement with a vow made in the darkness of despair.

The events that led up to the proceeding were these: I was staying in the West Country for a fortnight's trout fishing at the end of April. Several days had passed like some pleasant dream. The weather had been perfect, and the trout of the country fairly amenable, so that evening I was able to display a half-pounder or so, besides the ordinary tale of takeable fish – they ran about five to the pound – and one of half a pound was an achievement.

Therefore, lulled into a kind of false security, I was ill-prepared for the day when adversity came rushing against me on the wings of a northerly gale. I started by trudging four miles in wading stockings and brogues, a tedious form of exercise. But the day before, while taking a Sunday stroll, I had seen a perfectly monstrous trout, four pounds if an ounce, and he had decided my movements for the Monday. However, when the four miles were covered, I found that the wind was tearing straight down the valley, and making it quite impossible to get a fly at him. He had to be approached from below, for overhanging trees almost met above his haunt, and no wet fly line could be cut into the teeth of the wind.

I therefore did not attempt to cover him but waited

until there should come a lull, and, in the meantime, began to fish downstream with three flies. I never had a great deal of skill in downstream fishing, and I was not surprised when almost at once a good trout robbed me of the second dropper. Nor was I surprised when, on searching for the damping box, in which I had put some spare flies to soften the gut, I found that it had been left behind.

Accidents of this kind will happen, so I shrugged my shoulders, took out my fly book, and began to disentangle half a dozen Greenwell's glories, which had got themselves into hopeless confusion. After a good deal of patient work I extricated one and put the gut into my mouth. Then the other five blew away and vanished utterly. As they represented my remaining stock of this valuable fly, I spent half an hour in looking for them. Then I shrugged my shoulders once more, fastened on the dropper, and returned to the fishing. In less than a minute my last Greenwell was gone in another fish. The fly book was open once more, and a blue upright was taken out, while three red palmers were blown out, never to be seen again – by me, at all events.

Looking for them, however, occupied a certain amount of time, and it was fully twenty minutes before I got to fishing again. So far I had been content to let my line float out with the wind and settle on the water where it would; but now I desired to reach an eddy behind a big stone close to the opposite bank. To this end I attempted a cast across the wind, and failed utterly. A collar of three flies wrapped around one is an awkward thing to deal with, especially if, as in my case, the tail fly is fixed in a wading sock, the first dropper in the landing net, and the second in the small of one's back. It took me some time to rearrange matters, to replace the second dropper, which broke when I was taking off my coat, and to hunt for the four red spinners that I had the misfortune to lose when I opened my fly book.

But at last I got to work again, and began to realise that, in spite of the gale, the fish were rising in a remarkable manner. Almost every time the flies touched the water I could feel a pluck, but never a fish hooked himself or allowed me to hook him, until at last a big fellow took the tail fly with a plunge.

There may be men who, during a gale, can control a three-quarter pound trout at the end of a long line downstream in rough water on gossamer gut, but I am not one of them, and very soon I was searching for the six hare's ears that been blown out of my book while I was selecting a new tail fly. I did not find them, and there is no need for me to describe the search. It resembled the searches that had preceded it and those that came after.

Never in my life have I lost so many flies in one morning, and I believe that I have never seen and lost a greater number of fish. They seemed madly on the feed, and had it been only possible to fish upstream, I am certain I should have made a big basket. As it was I pricked trout, played them, lost flies in them, and did everything but land them. Finally, I left a whole cast in a bush over deep water, and retired from the unequal contest. I judged it well to give myself time to get calm, if that were possible, so I withdrew to the foot of the moorland hill, sat down with my back to the river, and endeavoured to think of Job. It seemed to me that I could have comforted him a little by contrasting his case with mine, although I did not see where any comfort was to come from for me. But by meditating on one's wrongs I suppose one gets comforted automatically, and presently I plucked up enough spirit to eat my sandwiches, and they did me good.

The discovery that I had left my flask behind with the damping box seemed but a slight thing in comparison with the tremendous evils of the morning, and I drank resignedly a draught of pure water from a rill trickling through the moss. After this I began to realise that the wind had dropped a little, and at once thought of my four pounder. If only he could be caught, the rest did not matter. A new cast was selected and soaked in the rill, and to it I attached a good big March brown. Then I returned to the river, and made my way upstream to the monster's haunt. He lay at the head of a long still pool, and from watching him the day before I had gathered that he moved up into the ripple to feed, and that he had a certain beat. I intended, therefore, to fish carefully up this beat, trusting to find him somewhere along it.

The wind was now considerably abated, and by wading along one side under the bushes, and casting across and upstream, it was possible to cover the necessary expanse of water. This I proceeded to do, and as this is a tale of woe there is no need to dwell on details. The fish, or a fish of great size, at any rate, was just where I expected, took the fly with a rush, ran out twenty yards of line, leaped twice, ejected the fly, and was gone in about half a minute, leaving me to my thoughts of Job and his exaggerated griefs.

After this I wandered upstream for a long way without troubling to fish until the crowning misfortune of the day fell upon me. For some distance the river had run through open moorland, but now I came to a field and surmounted a stile. Halfway across I became aware of approaching thunder, and, looking around, perceived that a herd of cattle was stampeding in my direction, apparently of set purpose. To avoid unprofitable argument, I stepped hurriedly down the steep bank into the river, which was just not deep enough to overtop my waders. The cattle reached the bank above, and watched me with indignation as I began to make my way across.

Then, as though by concerted arrangement, a fresh enemy appeared on the other side – a big, evil-looking black dog, which had the air of one accustomed to protect homesteads. It stood and waited for me in grim silence.

Then it was that I took the solemn oath to give up fishing, not only for that day, but for all time, if only I should win safely out of my parlous situation. I have no doubt that there was nothing to fear from either dog or cattle, but my nerves were upset by calamity. The rest is a tale of splashing downstream until I got back to the moor below the cattle and away from the dog. Incidentally, I broke the top of my rod and filled my waders, and had to walk home in dire discomfort and in heavy rain. As to the solemn oath, it was kept for a whole day. The day after, however, was the perfection of fishing weather, and the river had fined down nicely.

H. T. Sheringham, *An Open Creel,* 1910

Triumph, Then Tragedy

MUCH WATER has eddied under the bridges foamed over the weirs and lost itself in the Severn Sea since first I came under the spell, but the water must flow longer and stronger yet to wash away recollection of that solemn time.

It was high summer on Shakespeare's stream and afternoon – poetically it was always afternoon in the lotus land where white canvas alone shut out the stars at night but on this occasion prosaically also for luncheon was over and done with – when from afar I first espied a loggerhead chub basking at ease just outside the spreading willow.

No novice was I at the sport of angling, but had taken as many a brave fish as most boys of my years, with now and again a pounder among them, while I boasted acquaintance with a veteran angler who had that summer slain a cheven of full two pounds.

But here was something that passed my experience – a chub of unparalleled magnitude in a land where the community spoke with respect of pounders. He had length, breadth, and dignity; he lay at the surface, an imposing bulk, and for a while I stood spellbound. Then the natural boy asserted itself, and sought a plan of campaign. Now you must know that cheven is, in some respects, the wisest of fishes, and when he suns himself at the top he is impatient of intruders.

But a glimpse of Piscator or of the angle rod outlined against the sky, and he is gone, sunk quietly out of sight and reach. Strategy, therefore, demands that Piscator should grovel, trailing the angle rod behind, into some concealed position, whence the fly may be artfully despatched. Like the earthworm, I wriggled down the grassy slope to the little bush that offered the only bit of cover on the bank, and, peeping round it, found to my relief that the loggerhead was still in view.

But he was a long way off, twenty yards at least, and even had I been able to cast so far with the little nine-foot rod – 'suitable to youths' – and the light line, there was the rising ground behind to frustrate me. There was nothing for it but to wait in the hope that the fish might come a little nearer. So I waited, and I will not say that a prayer was not breathed to Poseidon that he should send the loggerhead towards my bank.

A long time I waited – maybe half an hour or more

– and the fish never moved more than an inch or two, but at long last he seemed to wake up. Some trifle of a fly attracted his attention, and I saw capacious jaws open and shut, and afterwards he seemed anxious for more, for he began to cruise slowly about. Then by slow degrees the circles of his course widened, until finally he was within about twelve yards of my bank. Now, I judged, was the time, and with a mighty effort and heart in mouth I switched out the fly at the end of my line (an artificial bluebottle, I remember) as far as I could. It fell quite a yard short, but that mattered little. Round he came sharply to see what had happened, steadily he swam up to the bluebottle, boldly he opened his mouth, and then I drank indeed the delight of battle.

Three pounds he weighed, all but an ounce, which doesn't matter, and for quite a time I fondly preserved his skin, adequately peppered and salted, as I thought, but in the end elders and betters intervened with forcible remarks about nuisances. So I was left with his memory only, of which nobody could rob me.

From that day I have revered the chub, and so often as the hot summer days come around so often do I bethink me of the sunlit waters, the cool willow shades, the fresh scent of waterweeds from the weir, the hum of bees, and, above all, the dark forms lying on the surface ready for the fly.

Some there are who will give you hard words concerning the chub, having, maybe, hooked him on Wye just in the V of the currents where they fondly expected a salmon, having perchance frayed the gossamer trout – cast all to tatters in keeping his brute strength out of the roots, and having disturbed twenty good yards of water to boot. But these unfortunates (I grant them the title) have encountered cheven out of his proper sphere, and their sympathies are warped thereby. Heed them not, but seek him in his rightful rivers, slow-flowing, rush-lined, lily-crowned, girt with willows and rich pastures; take with you your stoutest single-handed fly rod, strong gut, and big palmer flies, or Coachman, alder, Zulu – it matters little so the mouthful be big and so it have a small cunning tail of white kid; go warily along the bank with eye alert for a dark form under yon clay bank, in that little round hole among the lilies, beneath that tree, above that old log – anywhere, in fact, where a worthy fish may combine ease with dignity and, possibly, nutriment.

Having found him, pitch your fly at him with as much tumult as you please; if he does not see you or the rod, two to one he will rise. If he does see you he is gone, and herein lies most of the fascination of it. A stiff neck and a proud stomach are of no use to the chub fisher, who must stoop if he wishes to conquer.

With good luck you should catch a three-pounder, among others; with very good luck a four-pounder. Those who are what Horace Walpole, I believe, called serendipitous catch a five-pounder now and again. The favoured of the gods get a six-pounder once in their lives. And one or two anglers, for whose benefit the whole cosmic scheme has evidently been arranged, have caught a seven-pounder. But this last prodigy does not, I fancy, reward fly-fishing, though I once – but the memory of that giant lost cheven is too bitter to be evoked.

Cheese paste is the thing for seven-pounders if you know of any such, and you can put a piece on the hook of your fly if you like. But you cannot throw it very far, the fishing is difficult, and I much doubt whether there are many seven-pounders in the real world.

Your basking chub is so imposing that one's estimate of his ounces is insensibly coloured by awe. I have ever been curious to know how big was the chub that Walton and his pupil gave to Maudlin the milkmaid. The only indication vouchsafed to us is that it was just such another as the first one, with a white spot on its tail, and that was the biggest of twenty – all lying together in one hole. From this slender store of evidence I deduce it to have been two and a half pounds, because that is commonly the doyen in so numerous a shoal. The monsters do not often crowd so close as a score together. Four- and five- pounders are, I think, to be observed four or five in company, not more. How it may be with seven-pounders I know not; likely they swim in pairs, a pair to a mile of river, and that the best mile. I do not know of a pair, but I know of one that a good friend of mine captured in a recent year. It weighed seven pounds and a quarter, and constituted the gravest angling tragedy that has come under my notice in a decade, for the month was May, it was, of course, out of season and my friend is a very honest man. So the monster was gently returned, and some day will no doubt be the father of all the chub.

The loggerhead is a noble, pleasant fish, of thoughtful habit, and he gives right good sport to those who seek him with discretion, but he has, they say, his weak points. On the table – yet is this an angler's matter? All that concerns Piscator in the treatise of culinary wisdom is surely the first injunction, 'first catch him'. Caught, I have never found him otherwise than welcome to the descendants of sweet-throated Maudlin. It needs to inquire no further.

The finest sport I have ever had with chub was on a kind of April day set by accident in the middle of August, yet even this red letter day had an end to it that spoiled much of my pleasure. But let me take you through that day.

The wind blew with a certain amount of vehemence from the south-west; it was none too warm, and the lights and shadows caused by alternation of sunshine and cloud were far more suggestive of spring than of summer. It would have been an excellent day for trout, but it hardly promised great sport with chub. Still, the fortnight of August that had preceded this April day had provided no chub weather worth mentioning. What sun there had been was of pale and watery complexion, with great cloudbanks hovering near, ready to obscure him if he showed any sign of cheerfulness at all. The wind also had been cold and violent, and fly-fishing had been a mockery. The April day, therefore, was at least an improvement, and the split cane rod was put together with more cheerfulness of spirit. It would not be a case of stalking fish scientifically, for they would hardly be on the surface; but there was a chance that a big fly thrown into likely spots might bring up a brace or two of decent chub, and give the angler something to show for his pains. In these incredulous days it is sadly necessary to have something to show, and I was growing a little tired of explaining to the lay mind that success cannot be commanded when the weather is unpropitious. Besides, it is thankless work giving explanations that are obviously misunderstood.

Accordingly, I was resolute to catch something when I reached the bridge that spanned the Thames – here a mere infant river – with two small arches. Under the bridge the stream rippled in a manner provokingly suggestive of trout; but although there is much water that might well hold a head of *fario* in the topmost reaches of the river, the head of *fario* is conspicuously wanting.

A trout has occasionally been taken as high as this, but Lechlade, a good deal lower down, is the first point where the fish becomes a calculable possibility. Beyond regretting this fact, therefore, I took no thought of trout, but looked upstream for a sign of rising chub.

Above the sharp water at the bridge is a long, quiet pool, and in its lower corner, on the left bank, is a clump of bushes growing right down into the water, and forming a splendid harbour. A rise was soon seen just below the bushes, and then another, and presently it became evident that the fish were moving. Leaving the bridge, I got into the meadow opposite, from which it was possible to attain a small strip of shingle below, and within casting distance of the bushes. Before the edge was approached, however, some twenty yards of line were pulled off the reel and anointed with deer's fat. Since the chub were rising, they might just as well be attacked with a dry fly.

This is, perhaps, an unnecessary refinement for chub; and, indeed, it is not by any means always that they will take a floating fly properly, but when they do the sport is not to be despised. Preparations complete, and a biggish Coachman oiled and attached to a cast that tapered to the finest undrawn gut, the river was approached, and the attack begun.

The strip of shingle was about fifteen yards from the last bush, and the distance was soon found. Then the fly dropped close to the submerged twigs. There was no delay on the part of the chub, for a heavy fish plunged at the Coachman the instant it touched the water.

So sudden was the response that the line was not released by the fingers holding it against the rod butt, and a vigorous strike proved too much for the gut. Another plunge, and the chub was gone with the Coachman. This was vexatious, for the loss of a fish that has been hooked generally frightens the shoal. The rule is not quite invariable, however, so another fly was put on and cast a little higher up, in the hope that the other chub might not have noticed the little contretemps. This seemed to be the case, for a rise followed immediately. There was no mistake about the strike this time, and the reel screamed as the hook went home, continuing to scream as the fish dashed off. A chub's first rush is formidable, and with fine gut it is no good trying to stop it; but if the fish does not break, then it ought to be landed safely and speedily.

Before long the fight was over, and a fish of one and a half pounds was in the net, tapped on the head, and thrown out into the meadow, where the creel had been left. Then the fly was again thrown towards the bushes. Another fish took it immediately, and was landed in the same manner as the first, to which it might have been a twin brother. Then two smaller ones, of about one and a quarter pounds, each came to the net, and were returned.

In a good chub river nothing under one and a half pounds is really worth keeping, unless local taste in the matter of fish diet is very responsive; but big chub will sometimes find grateful recipients in the country.

After the brace of small ones had been returned, a two-pounder was landed, and after that several more fish of about one and a half pounds. By the end of half an hour there must have been a dozen or more landed and returned, and the sport showed no sign of slackening. Another two-pounder was just in the net when an exclamation was heard from the bridge. A cyclist had paused to look on, and was much impressed with the sight of somebody actually catching something. 'What a beauty!' he said, as yet another chub was landed. This remark suggested that a heaven-sent opportunity was at hand.

'Would you care for some fish?' I asked guilelessly. The cyclist nodded with strange enthusiasm, and was warmly pressed to help himself to the few bigger fish I had kept. He clambered down over the wall with his mackintosh cape, into which he packed the fish with some grass. He was full of gratitude at being told to take them all, and departed, bearing several pounds of chub at his saddle-bow, and leaving me to reflect that appreciation of true merit is hard to find, but when found, pleasant to contemplate.

After he had gone, fishing was resumed. A fish plunged at the Coachman, but would not take it. It was so obviously bigger than anything caught so far that it seemed worthwhile to change the fly, and several patterns were tried in vain. At last a wet fly, a big alder, with a wash leather tail, was put on, and cast in with a plop just where the fish had risen. A wave came out from the bushes at once, the line tightened, and a gentle strike fastened the hook into something better worth catching. The fish showed plenty of fight, but after one rush under the

twigs, from which a steady strain brought it out, there was no real danger, and before long a plump three-pounder was landed. He was deemed worthy of a place in the big creel, and was accordingly put in. After this, sport with the wet fly was quite as brisk as it had been with the coachman, and the fish were bigger – nothing under two pounds, and the biggest weighing three and a half pounds.

To sum up, by the time the rise was over the creel was full to the brim. All these fish had been caught without moving from the strip of shingle, and without fishing more than fifteen yards of water, which only shows how chub may be caught when they are really on the feed.

But my last cast provoked a curious – some might say unfortunate – conclusion to what should have been a wonderful morning. A massive chub followed the fly. I hooked it and for no reason I could ever understand, the hook fell out and the best chub I have ever seen escaped where all his fellows had succumbed. It is always the fish we lose that we remember, not the bag we take home.

I threw out the fly once more; a fish took it, and was played to the net, when it proved to be a small pike of about two and a half pounds. It gave a last kick as the net was about to receive it, the frayed gut parted, and my lucky fly, that glorious Coachman that had caught so many fish, vanished for ever.

H. T. Sheringham, *An Open Creel,* 1910

Chapter 7

TRAGIC MUSE

Mad About Pike

NOW THERE IS nothing remarkable in seeing a rod and reel in Ireland, but these particular weapons made me open my eyes and mouth in amazement. The rod at its point was thick as my little finger, the reel not less than eight inches in diameter and the line – shades of Izaak Walton! What a line was there. I have towed a canoe up the Thames with cord less thick. I was on the point of enquiring into the particular uses of this remarkable tackle, when the door of the cabin opened and a short, wiry old man with deep set, piercing eyes, iron grey hair and clad in a shabby suit of tweeds, came in wearily, bearing just such another rod and reel and a huge basket that I instinctively felt contained fish. He took no notice of me, but gasped out, in a voice that told of his exhausted condition: 'The steelyard, the steelyard!'

With trembling hands, he opened the rush basket and turned out of it one of the largest pike I had ever seen. Mrs O'Day, who seemed in no way surprised, produced an ancient rusty instrument and proceeded in a businesslike manner to weigh the fish. The old man's excitement while she did this was painful to witness.

'Is it? Is it?' he commenced.

'No, it isn't,' said Mrs O 'Day calmly. 'He's five pounds short.'

I was looking at the fish, but, hearing a groan, turned my eyes to the old fisherman and saw him lying on the floor of the cabin. He had fainted.

'Poor old man,' said Mrs O'Day. 'It's disappointed he is and weak too for devil a bit of food has he touched this day since yesterday. Undo his collar sir, and I'll mix him a timperance drink.'

And so her tongue ran on. Meanwhile, the old fellow came to himself and sat up, but his eyes went at once to the pike, which still lay on the floor. 'Only thirty-five pounds, I heard him mutter to himself.' But I will have him soon. I will have him soon. Mrs O'Day's timperance drink was in the nature of an egg flip. It acted like a charm on the old man, who five minutes after drinking it rose, kicked the fish to the side of the cabin and for the first time appeared to be aware that a stranger was in the shebeen. Mrs O'Day noticed the questioning look he cast at her.

'It's a gentleman who lost his way in the bog,' she said.

'Not fishing?' he asked rather anxiously.

'No, snipe shooting,' said I, and he seemed to me greatly relieved at the intelligence. Mrs O'Day now turned out the stew on to a large dish and apologised for having no plates, remarking that she was 'not used to the gentry'. We were both of us more or less famished and talked but little during the meal, after which, Mrs O'Day having provided us with a second edition of the 'timperance' drink, we drew the settle close to the peat fire, and commenced to chat over our pipes.

My new acquaintance, from what I could gather, was an Englishman who had lived for many years in Ireland and apparently passed his whole time in fishing. But I was able to tell him of certain modern methods of pike fishing of which he had heard nothing. By and by he began to get communicative and finally I ventured to ask him why the weighing of the pike had so disturbed him. Without hesitation he told me the following story.

'From a boy … I was an enthusiastic fisherman, I need not trouble to tell you how I caught salmon in Norway, gudgeon in the Thames, trout in the Test, and enormous grayling in the Hampshire Avon. I fished whichever and wherever I could and nothing, however large or however small, came amiss to me. But one thing I had never caught – a really large pike. Even in Sweden I never took one over thirty pounds.

'This nettled me, for many were the tales I read of monsters, particularly in the Irish lakes. One morning I read in a sporting paper a letter from an Irishman – a tackle dealer so I afterwards ascertained – asking why English anglers did not come more over there. In the lakes in his neighbourhood there was fine pike fishing. Thirty-pounders were common, and they got a forty-pounder or two every season. Here was exactly the information I wanted. I told some friends about it, but they only smiled. I said I would catch a forty-pounder before long. They replied that there was no such thing as a forty-pounder, alive or stuffed. Well, the end of it was I made a bet that I would go to Ireland and before I returned I would catch a fish of that weight.'

I here interrupted his story to tell him of a strange coincidence. It was that very tacklemaker's letter that had first brought me to Ireland. 'But go on,' I said, 'finish your story and then you shall have mine.'

'I began badly, he continued, 'I wrote to the man for details of these loughs he mentioned and received a reply from his widow, he having died soon after writing the paragraph. From the poor woman I could get no information. She said she had no idea to which waters her husband referred; in fact, she knew of none. Then I put a letter of enquiry in the sporting papers and received many replies from persons, some of whom were possibly not altogether disinterested in the matter.'

'I have suffered in the same way myself,' I interjected.

'I came to Ireland armed with tackle such as would

hold the largest pike that ever lived,' he continued, not noticing my interruption.

'At first I was hopeful. What tales they told me to be sure. There was one of a big pike caught in Lough Derg or, I should say, was killed by some workmen who were digging drains near the lake. The bishop of Killaloo was reputed to be fond of pike, and to him the fish was taken. It was so large that half its body dragged on the ground as two men carried it, slung on a pole, to the bishop's palace. When the bishop saw it, he told them to give it to the pigs. 'I am fond of pike,' said he, 'but distinctly decline to have anything to do with sharks.' Ah! What would I not have given to have caught that fish.

'Well, I fished here and I fished there, first trying all the large Shannon Lakes, and then visiting Corrib and Cullen. Thence I went to the north of Ireland, catching now and then some fine fish, but never even a thirty-pounder. The more difficult I found it to attain my object, the more determined I became to succeed. And I shall succeed yet. Let me see. It is now twenty-five years since I came to Ireland. I must have caught thousands of pike in that time – that one there on the floor is the largest of the lot; in fact, the largest I have seen caught by myself or anybody else. This is my second great disappointment.

'At Athlone I thought I had succeeded. That was a big fish. I took him to the station and weighed him there. Forty-three pounds, said the station master. A Major Brown who was looking on began to prod the fish with his stick. 'Something hard there,' he said. 'Let's cut him open and see what he had for dinner.' I would not agree to this as I wanted the skin entire, but the major squeezed him a bit and up came a lot of swan shot that my scoundrel of a boatman had evidently poured down his throat so that he might earn the reward I had promised him if I caught a heavy fish.

'But at last I really have found a monster pike – the catching of him is only a question of time. Not a quarter of a mile from this cabin,' here he lowered his voice to a whisper, 'is a deep reedy lake. The priest has a boat on it, which he lends me. I was rowing along the other evening when something struck the boat with such force that I was thrown from the seat and nearly capsized. It was in deep water and there are no rocks in the lake. I had rowed right on to a pike as large as a calf.'

He said the last sentence slowly and earnestly. I expect I showed great interest in the statement for, like the old man, it had long been my ambition to catch a really immense pike.

'Well,' said I, 'let us go and try the lake together. I should like to help you land such a monster.'

'Ah, but you might catch him and not I. How then?'

And he gave me a very unpleasant look out of his deep-set eyes. We said nothing for a while, when my companion suddenly startled me by asking if I was aware that he was the Emperor of Germany. I said I was not, and another unpleasant silence ensued.

Mrs O'Day had made up two heather beds for us on the mud floor and without undressing we each stretched ourselves on our moorland couches. Just as I was dropping off to sleep, my companion got up on his elbow and said gravely: 'Hang me if I don't believe you are a pike. I'll have a triangle into you tomorrow morning. Good night.'

There was no doubt about it. His disastrous obsession had driven him mad. I dared not go to sleep. I made a pretence of it until the old man began to snore and then sat by the fire until daybreak when, leaving some money on the table for Mrs O'Day, I sped away over the moor.

Years afterwards I was telling the tale of the demented angler who, I felt certain, had lost his wits in his unavailing search after a big Irish pike, when I was interrupted by Rooney, of the Irish Bar, who burst into a peal of laughter, swearing that he knew my pike-fishing acquaintance well and that there was no saner man in Ireland.

'Fact is Johnny,' said he, 'the old boy was fearful you would get that big fish before him and so he thought he would frighten you home.'

Rooney may say what he likes, but I decline to believe in the sanity of any man who expatriates himself during a quarter of a century in the endeavour to catch a forty-pound pike.

John Bickerdyke, *Wild Sport in Ireland,* 1895

Fish Attacks Boy

ONE OF MY SONS, aged fifteen, went with three other boys to fish and to bathe in Inglemere Pond, near Ascot racecourse, and nearly lost his leg. This is how the terrible event unfolded. He walked gently into the water to about the depth of four feet when he spread out his hands to attempt to swim.

Instantly a large fish came up and took his hand into his mouth as far up as the wrist, but, finding he could now swallow it, relinquished his hold, and the boy, turning around, prepared for a hasty retreat out of the pond. His companions, who saw it, also scrambled out of the pond as fast as possible.

My son had scarcely turned himself around when the fish came up behind and immediately seized his other hand crosswise, inflicting some very deep wounds on the back of it. The boy raised his first-bitten and still bleeding arm, and struck the monster a hard blow on the head, then the fish disappeared, but not before making a savage slash at his leg that inflicted deeper wounds even than those on his hands.

The other boys assisted him to dress, bound up his hand and leg with their handkerchiefs as best they could, and brought him home. We took him down to Mr Brown, surgeon, who dressed seven wounds in one hand and two much more serious wounds in his leg; and so great was the pain the next day, that the lad fainted twice;

the little finger was bitten through the nail and it was more than six weeks before it was well. The nail came off and the scar remains to this day.

Reading Mercury, June 1856

Double Disaster

IT WAS a Sunday evening. As the end of the week drew near we had been anxious as to local customs with regard to Sunday fishing – these varying in different parts of Norway. Erik had told us we might fish after dinner; and Gjertrud, our laughter-loving handmaiden who happily seemed to find something comical in almost everything we said and did, propounded the brilliant idea.

Yes, but you can dine at ten and begin fishing at eleven o'clock. There was subtlety about this capable of infinite development, but it struck us as too refined, so we delayed starting until four in the afternoon; the greater population of the village, we observed, accompanying us or making short cuts through the woods.

When I commenced to cast over the Stein Pool from the platform, there was an audience of thirty-four folks, lads and lassies, old men and maidens, assembled on the bank behind.

Stein Pool is dead and deep, with a moderate stream running in beyond mid-river, and the fish lying well in towards the opposite bank, which was heavily wooded down to the brink. The nearer half of the river is (in fine water) a deep black set where the line, if allowed to enter, is instantly drowned. This combination necessitates not only long casting, but rapid long throws and quick returns, which means hard work, especially as a high bank, twenty yards behind, involved lifting the line well up in the air.

The swish of the line in the faces of the spectators soon cleared them off to safer distances, and about halfway down the pool there came that tug – no, it is not a tug, but a sudden inflexible resistance as of a tree trunk or solid rock. But I knew that a big fish had annexed the fly, deep under and without showing, and delayed not to drive the small double hook well home into his jaws.

Five minutes later, after a prolonged period of bottom fighting, jagging and sulking, alternated with sub-aquatic gymnastics and contortions that kept me trembling for my tackle the captive came up with a sudden rush to the surface, ploughing along on his bent broadside for twenty yards. Then we saw that this fish was even bigger than the lost monster of Samkomme.

Was it possible to subdue such a salmon on that paltry hook? True, it was a double; that reflection seemed inspiring. But then the hooks were smaller than that which had already failed, being actually the smallest (No. 5) in all my collection and therefore specially selected for fine water in a streamless pool. I determined rightly or wrongly to play for safety, to act solely on the defensive, and to leave the fish to exhaust himself, even though it involved my spending the night with him in the process.

I pass over details which would involve repetition. Suffice it that the fish, persistently dropping downstream, obliged me to follow. This for some distance was easy enough, but lower down trees grew to the water's edge. Still it was necessary to follow, having some fifty yards of line out.

The fish was now in the shallows, rolling heavily at intervals with short, sullen rushes, during one of which I felt a slight draw – perhaps the hold of one hook had failed. W., going down through the trees to reconnoitre, reported the fish tired. For almost minutes at a time he lay inert in midstream, suffering himself to be towed ahead in the slack pool tail without resistance.

Had it now been possible to incline the rod inland, an opportunity to net him might, it seemed probable, be secured. But the thickset branches projecting far across the stream forbade this and two alternatives remained.

One was to drop still lower downstream trusting to find shallows and get in the cleek at the foot of the pool. This, however, I rejected, first, because the fish was yet in no sense under control and the danger in the stronger stream obvious, nor was there any reasonable certainty of netting there. Secondly, because I knew nothing of the depth or nature of the water below, beyond seeing that there was a strong rapid at least two hundred yards long with an island in midstream and thick wood on either bank. Hence, I elected the other course, and endeavoured slowly to tow the half-beaten fish upstream and thus clear the trees. A stone thrown in below the fish's tail at this point might have served the purpose, but we did not think of it at the time. While thus engaged, although exerting no special pressure – indeed, humouring the captive in all his little runs and lunges – the rod flew up and the fly came home unharmed. The fight was over and the fish the victor. Never had I felt that such a disappointment had come upon me.

A few days after in the Stein Pool, I hooked yet another monster. I felt him come and struck at the right moment, yet in rather less than a minute, for some reason unexplained, the hook came away.

During his short captivity he had made one long surface run, thus showing up his size. The conclusions we came to were these. That these very heavy fish given the best of holds on single gut may take an hour to land and possibly more, and that during so long a pressure the hold of a small hook (in fine water no other is of any use) must almost necessarily wear itself out. I give for what it may be worth, the quality and rank of the two above named fish, these points being set down by estimate by the local experts.

1. The Samkomme fish, forty pounds, fresh from sea the night before.
2. The Stein Pool fish, a larger salmon, probably from forty to fifty, but of some fourteen days' sojourn in the river.

These estimates I take to be fairly near the mark. After landing heavy fish one comes to know the strength and style of the twenty-pounder and of fish ranging between that and thirty pounds. There are old hands among anglers who never fail to land a fish. They may smile at this record of disaster, pointing out things done that should have been avoided, or neglected that should have been tried. Well, to criticise is easy; so, too, is it to haul out heavy but ill-conditioned autumn fish from the depths of some sluggish hole. But with fresh-run springers in Scandinavian streams the case is different and the difficulty greater and more varied.

Abel Chapman, *Wild Norway*, 1897

Tackle Dancing Bull

I WAS once fishing a good grayling river and failed to notice – probably because I was wading at the time and had caught several good fish – that a large and very fierce bull had been watching me for some time. By the time I, happily casting from my position midstream, noticed the bull I couldn't get back to my tackle. The bull was about ten feet away from my favourite fish basket, tackle bag and spare rod. Worse, the basket contained several very good grayling. I did not like the prospect of losing any of these things, but what was I to do.

Attack being the best form of defence, I decided to wade a little further downstream, quietly come ashore and then try to frighten the bull away. The first part of the plan succeeded. I reached the bank about thirty feet downstream of the bull, which still seemed intent on goings on in the middle of the river. I found an old half-rotten piece of fence post and a couple of large clods of earth. I threw them at the bull while bellowing all kinds of dire threats. The bull turned, looked at me and charged. I beat a hasty retreat, but this time across a rickety wooden bridge by which I'd been standing. To my astonishment the bull attempted to cross and reversed off the footbridge only when it began to sway violently under his enormous weight.

Outmanoeuvred, the bull let out a roar and trotted back to my vulnerable looking pile of tackle. Here, to my lifelong astonishment, it began to do a sort of crazy war dance on top of rods, basket and box.

In a few moments my favourite gear was reduced to a crunched and broken pile of fragments. My fish had been mashed into the mud, my basket and box smashed beyond repair. My favourite rod was in at least fifteen pieces. Then, honour satisfied, the bull trotted off to a distant part of its field and left me to pick up the pieces and set off for home.

J. H. R. Bazeley, *Fishing Stunts,* 1919

Night Manoeuvres

SOME FISHERMEN are very keen on night fishing, but I do not envy them in the least for, although large fish can be caught in the dark, the pleasure of playing the fish is entirely lost.

I remember one very hot dry summer when there was little or nothing doing in the daytime a fellow angler persuaded me one dark night to go fishing with him. We started at 10pm to a spot on the river where it was shallow on one side and deep on the other. We used a fairly large light brown fly and thick gut, waded in about a yard and sent the fly on the water in front; but the difficulty was to see how much line to put out without hitting the far bank; the only way to see was by stooping down so as to see the reflection on the face of the water.

After a few throws I hooked a big fish, which made off downstream; after much time and with much trouble I dragged it ashore and with much further trouble (neither of us had brought an electric torch) managed to get the hook out. The result (till one in the morning) was three fish between us and my waders spoilt by thorn bushes in the rough ground on the way back.

On another occasion I was persuaded to go sea trout fishing and after three hours got one fish. This time I left my waders at home and with an electric torch selected a place I thought good, sat on an old tin pail and kept throwing the fly. As the sea trout would only just nibble the fly it meant striking directly the nibble was felt; result one sea trout and loss of several flies and casts.

One night I went eel fishing, taking a lantern, and a newspaper to drop the eel on when caught as it could be seen and could not wriggle away quickly. It was a very dark night, weird and windy and the rats or water rats were continually passing around me, no doubt attracted by the lantern. However, we caught many eels, not bothering to extract the hooks but simply cutting the line.

It was after midnight when I made my last cast, using a big worm. After a while I heard a commotion in the water and the line was pulled out of my hand. I managed to seize the rod before that went and then a very heavy fish leaped out of the water and I saw by the glint of the scales on it that I had hooked a large salmon. As it was quite dark I could not move about and the line soon parted. It was certainly the best salmon I had ever hooked and I cursed myself for not thinking that hooking such a fish was always a possibility.

After these experiences I came to the conclusion that the game – meaning night fishing – was not worth the candle with the loss of flies, cast and waders, not being able to see to play the fish properly and being exhausted with want of sleep next day. The loss of that great salmon pains me to this day.

J. C. Eaton,
Seventy Years Observations of a Trout Fisherman, 1937

Fit for an Emperor

OUR WHOLE FAMILY went to Europe in the spring of 1883 when I was seventeen years old. My grandfather, Peter Cooper, had died that winter, and my mother wanted to get away. We spent the winter in Rome, where the climate did not agree with me, so that in the spring I had developed a very bad throat. As this did not get better with the warmer weather, my mother took me to a specialist in Paris, who recommended a course of waters at Bad Ems, in Germany. I was bundled off with my tutor, as I could prepare for college as well there as anywhere.

We stopped at a boarding house called the Vier Turme or Four Towers, at the end of the park, by the River Lahn. After I got into the routine of the cure and my study periods, I had spare time to amuse myself. The Lahn flowed through the centre of Ems, bordered by a fine park that rimmed the river with a stone wall. Just opposite the palace, where the Emperor stayed when taking the Waters, there was a stone landing stage for boats. All along the river I noticed men fishing, using cherries, and bread dough mixed with cheese, for bait. They said they were fishing for barbel. This fish looks like a sucker with catfish whiskers. They did not seem to be getting many fish, and I suspected that they had the wrong bait. It looked to me as if such a fish would be more likely to take worms.

One morning I dug some large worms in a flower bed near the Vier Turme and proceeded with my rod to the river at the boat landing before the palace, as I suspected the drain from the palace came into the river at this point. I baited on a large gob of worms and let it sink to the bottom, as these fish were sure to be bottom feeders.

The bait had not been long on the bottom when I felt a heavy pull and I was fast to a large fish. Those I had seen caught were small, but this was quite a different story. My little trout rod had all it could do to handle this big fish, but I finally got it up to the landing and took it by the gills and hauled it out, amid the plaudits of the crowd assembled along the stone wall and on the bridge farther up. I was about to hit the fish on the head to kill it, when an officer with his chest covered with medals touched me on the arm and signed to me not to kill the fish but to bring it along and follow him.

I was completely mystified and thought I had broken some law or other. He led me across the roadway, over to a large stone fountain before the palace and signed to me to put the fish in the water. Then he was all smiles and bowed me away.

I went back to my fishing still not understanding why my wonderful big fish had been taken away from me. It would have weighed about eight pounds I would guess; it was about thirty inches long.

I had not been fishing more than a half hour when the same officer came down to the landing again and touched me on the shoulder and signed for me to follow him and leave my rod. This time I was sure I was arrested and was quite scared. He led me over before two other men in military dress and saluted and stood at attention.

The elder of the two men addressed me in perfect English saying, 'I want to thank you for catching me the finest barbel I have ever seen for my breakfast, and I want to commission you to catch me one every day during my stay here.'

I then realised that this was Emperor William I speaking, and the man beside him was Fritz, the Crown Prince. I stammered out my thanks for the great honour and retired to my fishing as best I could. After that, for three weeks, the Emperor came down to my fishing place about ten o'clock every morning and asked if I had caught his fish that day. I nearly always got one or two, but never one as large as that first fish, which was the granddaddy of the river, evidently. Then the day came when I hooked a truly monstrous barbel but I could do nothing with him and after a short, one-sided battle the great fish was gone. I was crushed by this disaster. But still the emperor came to see me. Several mornings he asked me to walk with him a-ways in the park and he asked many questions about America, about which he was well informed. Twice, on these walks, Bismarck was with him. The old Emperor was always affable and pleasant, but Bismarck gave me the creeps even to look at him. He was the most forceful and sinister man I ever saw. But the great disappointment of my days on the river was that I had lost that big barbel; I know that if I had managed to land it the emperor would surely have invited me to the palace. Now that really would have been something!

Edward Hewitt,
A Trout and Salmon Fisherman for 75 Years, 1948

Eighty Pounder Lost

AS REGARDS to huge fish of more than fifty pounds, the first of which I have any record is the legendary monster that the Hon. Geoffrey Hill, and Christmas the keeper, played all through a summer night in the Agin Pool at the Nyth, but this fish was never even seen by the angler, and therefore cannot be included in any account of really big fish.

Nor can that other great fish that a medico of Ross played all night long, only to find in the morning that he had been anchored to a piece of fencing wire, the uneasy writhings of which had deceived him into believing they were the struggles of a salmon.

Five fish only of more than fifty pounds have been caught in the Wye on the rod, and the full list is as follows: the first of these huge salmon weighed fifty-one pounds and was caught by the late Mr. J. Wyndham Smith in 1914. He caught this salmon in the famous Quarry Pool at Aramstone; and on the same morning he killed another fish of forty-four pounds. Two fish weighing ninety-five pounds and this, I believe, a record for a single day's fishing in the Wye, as regards size.

In March, too, Colonel Tilney caught the second in Higgins Wood at Whitney, which weighed fifty-two pounds, and thereby set up a record for size that lasted for three years, until on 13 March, 1923, Miss Doreen Davey (now Mrs Pryce Jenkin) broke the record again in the Cowpond, with a fish of fifty-nine and a half pounds, and this record is still unbroken. I believe this is a spring record for Great Britain.

This was a magnificently proportioned salmon measuring fifty-two and a half inches in length and twenty-nine inches in girth. It looked like a massive side of bacon when lying on the slab and it gave her the fight of a lifetime before it came to the gaff.

Miss Davey's fish, monstrous as it was, pales into insignificance beside the huge and decaying corpse of a salmon that was found in the river at Even at Pitt Bridge on 26 May 1920. The previous history of this fish is very mysterious and the story has almost become a legend of the past. It is believed that this enormous salmon could have been the greatest fish ever from the river on rod and line had it not been lost after a tremendous battle. It was hooked in Lower Pike's at Whitney by General Davidson and played for a very long time until both fish and angler were exhausted.

At last a terrible thing happened; terrible and tragic: the trace broke and the gigantic salmon rolled away downstream. Nothing more was heard until sometime later, when an enormous salmon was found lying dead in the river near Hereford. The finder measured the salmon and found that it was no less than fifty-nine and a half inches long and thirty-three and a quarter inches in girth.

Measurements such as these would mean that the fish weighed in life about eighty pounds, but the mystery deepened further still. The finder went away, leaving the fish on the bank and meaning to return for it later. On his return the fish had disappeared.

Evidently someone had thrown it into the river, and in the river it remained until it was discovered in a liquefying rotten condition miles further down. Even when in this terrible state and falling to pieces, the fish measured fifty-seven inches long and twenty-six inches in girth.

Undoubtedly this is the biggest Wye salmon of which we have any record; had fate willed otherwise it could so easily have been landed after that epic battle and angler and fish would have been immortalised.

H. A. Gilbert,
The Tale of a Wye Fisherman, 1928

Clouded in Myth

EVEN ON THAT, bleak ugly day of northerly wind and colourless skies, the upper end of Corrib showed a fair challenge to Killarney. Thickly strewn with wooded islands, it is backed by ranges of bold mountain; but its chief charm lies in the romantic suggestion of the pass towards Maam, where its winding water, lost to sight between the cliff-like hills, tempts one to row continually onwards and explore what recesses may be enfolded among the gaunt crags that guard the entrance to the Joyces' country.

That day, however, we were due to lunch near Lord Ardilaun's fine house and famous woodcock covers, and so we kept close and wheeled about around rocks, aiming at the points where deep water fringes a shallow, and the big trout and pike cruise about looking for incautious fry.

Meanwhile, naturally, we talked about big trout; and it appeared that Tom Lydon had captured the show fish of the hotel, which, glossy in its glass case, had impressed me solemnly while I breakfasted. It weighed twelve pounds, he told me; and after it was sent to be stuffed he caught another half as big again. This fish, eighteen pounds, took a bait attached to a hand-line, and, as Lydon said, you could do nothing but throw the reel at him. It, being wooden, floated, of course, and the fish was eventually landed.

I listened as to a chapter of mythology, and in the meantime nothing happened. At last we turned homewards to lunch, and shortly after there was a pull at the rod, from which a wagtail was fishing; but this first fish proved to be only an inconsiderable pike. It broke the ice, though: five minutes later there came a savage pluck at the same line, and the moment I had the rod in hand I knew we were into something heavy.

Probably another pike, I thought, and sighed for waters where a big fish can be relied on to be a good fish. But at the next instant the unknown quantity made a short run – luckily crosswise, for his first race had nearly stripped my reel – and then foundered head and tail up.

At all events, here was no pike; the sickly yellow gleam did not show itself. I set him down for a salmon long up and discoloured, and the boatman found confirmation in the fact that he was now moving constantly upwind. We got the boat parallel with him, and I shortened line as quickly as I could, while Lydon exhorted me to handle him gently, for he was on the light trace.

We are accustomed to fish very light in the north of Ireland, and the mere thinness of the gut would not have terrified me; but when I thought of the local draper's shop, grave doubts – which I retract and apologise for – rose up in my mind.

Then suddenly, perhaps thirty yards off, the fish rose so high in the water that we could see him plainly; and his broad golden side was covered with huge black spots. Young Lydon shouted: 'It's no salmon; it's a splendid great trout.' But his father was more eloquent. Dropping his oar, he shifted his place to the bow. 'Maybe you'd better take the net,' he said to the son. I felt then that this was indeed a great occasion, when this hardy veteran would admit the advantage of youth.

Heavens above, how I wished that we had put our swivels into gut that commanded my confidence.

There are few incidents in the business of wearing down a heavy fish in a lake with light rod and tackle, but the strain on one's nerves is considerable when the prize is so uncommon as we knew this fish to be. Somewhere about ten pounds, I guessed him – at any rate, a bigger brown trout than my wildest ambitions had ever aspired to – and, contrary to all precedent, the nearer he came, the bigger he looked.

'He's fourteen pounds!' Johnny Lydon cried, when a great back showed for a moment above the water. Inwardly I set this down for exaggeration, but it added to my excitement that I had never seen experienced boatmen so eager and anxious. There was a continual fire of snapping injunctions from one to the other – generally speaking, instructions to do the thing that the man instructed had already begun to do. The boat in reality, and not I, was playing the fish; my part was only to keep an equable strain and watch that the reel kept absolutely clear.

We had come about half a mile with the fish, humouring him away from all dangerous possibilities of weed or rocky shallow; and another boat nearby had stopped fishing and pulled over to watch the event. We were all anxious; but luckily the old grilse rod's top was very limber, and I could be tolerably secure that no sudden plunge would meet with too much resistance. With an ordinary spinning rod and that trace the odds would have been on the fish; and as it was, the tackle was wholly too light to lift his head. Gradually, however, and most skilfully, the boat was sidled down. I had learned enough not to try to drag or force the fish, but rather to go to him.

Still, he kept sheering off from the side of the boat; and suddenly Johnny Lydon passed me and took up his position in the stern. It was an awful moment, for as he leant over he hid the line from me, and every angler knows that the eye, quicker even than the hand, tells when to ease off the strain and stop a heavy fish from floundering on the top of the water. But right or wrong, I left Lydon his own way, and kept up the strain through seconds that were like minutes, while he shouted his directions and the boat was backed quietly down.

One felt rather than saw when he lunged for the fish; and he had reached out so far that he paused for an instant to recover while the trout hung at the edge of the net.

Another lift, and it was in the boat at last. Lydon held it between his knees while he lifted an iron thole pin for a priest, gave a couple of decisive taps, and then laid it on the boards of the boat. If he was big in the water, he looked bigger now, for all of us gasped.

'Fifteen pounds,' I said. But the other boat drew over now and hailed us, and we did not venture to commit ourselves beyond thirteen or fourteen. This angler had scales, and lent them; and the pointer hung somewhere between sixteen and eighteen, as nearly as possible midway. It was a great moment. I never saw another fish weigh so much heavier than he was guessed at. The exact figure when we got him on kitchen scales was sixteen pounds — and I quoted it to someone the same evening. But Johnny Lydon looked at me with pained eyes. 'Sir, for the love of God, say seventeen pound.' And for the love at all events of Johnny Lydon, I have always used the nearest round figure to the truth. How many anglers can say as much?

That was my first trout on Corrib. Lydon of Galway told me he had seen one landed a pound heavier, and my boatman, as I have said, also had an eighteen-pounder to his credit; but these things happened a good while ago, and my piece of luck was portentous.

There is, of course, no question of skill in trailing a line behind a boat; and if it is true that in playing a salmon from the bank much depends on the net man, the same is far more emphatically to be said in the case of lake angling. This fish, as we happened to be able to determine, took from fifteen to twenty minutes to land, and he was netted before I ever got him on his side at all. With a less competent boatman I have been kept nearly an hour in landing a ten-pound salmon on tackle very little lighter. Consequently, it seems that we all had good reason to be pleased with one another, and certainly we were.

The rest of my day's fishing is of no interest. I landed altogether six fish: three trout (making twenty pounds), two small pike, and a large cannibal perch which took the minnow.

But the history of the big fish has sad ramifications. It was decided that he should be stuffed, and accordingly, when we went in to lunch at my friend's house on the lake, careful preparations were made to send him off and the fish reached Cong that afternoon in a well-secured box. We arrived not long after from the lake, and young Lydon announced the capture to the factotum of the hotel. He smiled pleasantly, and said, 'May be!'

Lydon grew eloquent and indignant, but I suggested that the hotel keeper should go down to the post office and heft the box. The proposal was scouted; of course he believed me implicitly. I went upstairs to my room, and approached the window in time to see this convinced person hot-foot to the post office. He came back in a wholly altered frame of mind, eager now for measurements. I gave them him: length, thirty-three and a half inches, by nineteen and a half inches girth, and the girth almost uniform over the whole body of the fish, which was extraordinarily deep behind the dorsal fin. But if I had been wise, or he had been wise, he would have had the box opened, and had a public display in the street of Cong. For on the day we were on Lough Mask and told our story there, only to be treated with the bare civility that is accorded to extravagant liars; and we returned to find word had reached the fourteen anglers fishing nearby from Clonbur, and that all fourteen had refused to believe because none of their informants had seen the fish.

On the day following, I departed, but a month later again passed through Cong. My carman met me some miles out, and at once launched out in copious Gaelic. There was not the like of such talk in Ireland as was on your trout. 'Arrah, why did you bring him to Cong in a box – and me getting my head broke over all the country!'

Last Wednesday, he went on to explain, he had been in Ballinrobe, 'and says one of the boatmen to me, "No such a trout was ever caught in Corrib."

'You're a liar,' says I to him, I seen it. And with that he struck me. An sure, sir, I never seen it at all; only what was I to say?

He quoted to me also the opinion of a certain captain. "Where is the man you say caught him?" says the Captain to me. 'Gone,' says I. "And it was Saturday you say he caught him, and this is Thursday. Don't tell me," says he. "A man that caught a fish like that would fish a month for the comrade."

So it is to be feared that my fish, although quite authentic, is somehow clouded in myth at the place of his capture. What's worse, the box the fish was sent in to be stuffed vanished and it was as if my giant had never been. Serve me right for not catching it on a fly but on a

line dragged behind a boat, a technique of no skill at all.
A waste of a rare giant.

Stephen Gwynne, *Duffer's Luck,* 1924